The Preppers Survival Handbook

The Essential Long-Term Step-By-Step Survival Guide to the Worst Case Scenario for Surviving Anywhere - Prepper's Pantry, Survival Medicine & First Aid

Buck Collins

Buck Collins

The Prepper's Survival Handbook

Buck Collins

© Copyright 2020 Survivr Source - All rights reserved.

The content contained within this book may not be reproduced, duplicated or transmitted without direct written permission from the author or the publisher.

Under no circumstances will any blame or legal responsibility be held against the publisher, or author, for any damages, reparation, or monetary loss due to the information contained within this book either directly or indirectly.

Legal Notice:

This book is copyright protected. This book is only for personal use. You cannot amend, distribute, sell, use, quote or paraphrase any part, or the content within this book, without the consent of the author or publisher.

Disclaimer Notice:

Please note the information contained within this document is for educational and entertainment purposes only. All effort has been executed to present accurate, up to date, and reliable, complete information. No warranties of any kind are declared or implied. Readers acknowledge that the author is not engaging in the rendering of legal, financial, medical or professional advice. The content within this book has been derived from various sources. Please consult a licensed professional before attempting any techniques outlined in this book.

By reading this document, the reader agrees that under no circumstances is the author responsible for any losses, direct or indirect, which are incurred as a result of the use of the information contained within this document, including, but not limited to, — errors, omissions, or inaccuracies.

Table of Contents

Legal Notice: 4

Disclaimer Notice: 4

Introduction **10**

    Preparation Mentality 11

    Our Responsibilities 13

    Pop Quiz 1 14

    Pop Quiz 2 17

Chapter 1 - Lessons from the Experts **19**

    Case Study 1: Disaster in New Orleans 20

    Case Study 2: A Calm Retreat 22

    Case Study 4: The Virtual Family Dinner 25

Chapter 2 - Food **28**

    Basal metabolic rate 28

    Hunkering Down 31

    The List: 33

    Noodles/Pastas 33

    Dried Grains 34

    Canned Beans/Meats 34

Canned Fruits/Veg 34

Dried Nuts/Fruits 35

Dried Meats 35

Milk/Dairy/Eggs/Alternatives 35

Baking/ Cooking Supplies 36

Fresh Fruit and Veg 37

Frozen Food 38

Vitamins and Minerals 38

Condiments/Spices 38

Drinks 39

Growing 43

Preserving 47

Bugging Out 52

Chapter 3 - Water 56

Chlorine Tabs 61

Boiling 62

UV Lights 62

Filtration 63

Squeeze filters/Life Straw 63

Pump filters 64

    Gravity filters 64

Chapter 4 - First Aid 65

    Dental Emergencies and Basic Care Kit 68

    PROCEDURE FOR CPR 77

    CPR FOR CHILDREN 79

    Hyperthermia 84

Chapter 5 - Children 90

Chapter 6 - Day-to-Day Needs 97

    Warmth 98

    Fire 99

    Illumination 99

    Navigation 100

    Sun Protection 100

    Entertainment 101

    Personal Hygiene: 101

    Cleaning: 104

    Maintenance: 106

    Special Considerations for People with Disabilities: 109

    For the Hearing Impaired: 112

    Developmental/ Sensory Challenges: 113

Chapter 7 - Mental Health Emergency Kit..............115

Chapter 8 - Recovery Work and Community Service 130

    Volunteer 133

    Join a Response Team..135

    Step One: Risk Assessment...136

    Step Two: Establish Protective Measures.........................137

    Step Three: Emergency Procedures 140

    Risk Assessment: 140

    Protective Measures: 140

    Storms: 140

    Flooding: 141

    Pandemics: 141

    Fire: 141

    Unrest: 142

    Emergency Procedures: 142

Summary and Check Lists....................................146

The Prepper's Survival Handbook

SPECIAL BONUS!

Want These 2 Bonus Books for FREE?

Get **FREE**, unlimited access to these and all of our new books by joining the Survivr Source Community!

SCAN w/ your camera TO JOIN!

9

Buck Collins

Introduction

So here we are, in the midst of a global pandemic. You're quarantined in your home somewhere in the world, feeling that eerie mix of calm and panic. It's a concoction that makes your throat dry and your chest feel like it's about to explode. Or are those just symptoms of something more sinister?

The grocery stores have been all but emptied. Your favorite bar was boarded up after some hooligans raided it two nights prior. There's a church ten blocks away still serving chicken stew in Styrofoam bowls, but the police are standing by, keeping people from trampling one another. The police are enforcing curfew now too. No one's allowed out of their homes unless it's on the way to the hospital... or the morgue. Things are bleak. Too bleak.

You're wondering if now is the time to start preparing for the end. You've got a few cans of expired ham and beans, some rotten-looking potatoes, and a purple onion that has lived in this apartment longer than you have. Well, people have survived on less, right?

What if you could rewind to the time just before people were panic-buying in your city? To the time when the news showed more than just the death toll. You might have found this book right on time. After all, it is never too late or too complicated, or too crazy to prepare. Preparation takes no more strength than going grocery shopping. Preparation takes no more time than it takes to fill a backpack. Preparation takes no more knowledge than it takes to flip a page.

In what follows, you will find a comprehensive guide to stocking your shelves, gathering your team, and steeling your mind. For you will find that preparation is all about mentality.

Preparation Mentality

Panic is a sickness. It kills more people than a virus or a fire or a flood ever could. Panic makes us think that guns are more important than food. It makes us trample over other people just to get to what we need. It makes us throw money at products or gadgets that we think might save us instead of learning how to take care of ourselves. Panic makes us stupid. Stupidity is deadly.

How do we avoid panic? The only cure for panic is preparation. If you have spent all your time thinking about solutions to hypothetical situations, then you are unlikely to fall victim to victimhood-mentality. Preparation is about being positive that you will have not only the necessities for survival, but also the purpose to move forward, the reason to keep pushing, keep adapting, keep thriving. Preparation ensures that your focus is always on how to make the most out of a bad situation, rather than facing that situation without any plan at all.

It is not outlandish, or conspiracy theorist, or overly zealous to prepare for a natural or manmade disaster. It is a basic facet of human evolution. In much the same way our predecessors had to prepare for a hunt or a war, you prepare for a job interview or an exam. We run scenarios through our mind, readying our body for the task at hand. The greatest test of our lives comes from the need to survive and if you are reading this then you understand your part to play in any extreme emergency.

It's not about trying to collect everything you can in a wild fear of what the future might bring. It's about focusing on what you can do in this moment to maintain health and normalcy regardless of the future. More than that though, it's about equipping yourself so that you can better serve your family, your friends, and your community.

Our Responsibilities

As a husband and father of four, I've come to know the importance of community and cooperation. My family has been a part of our local Prepper's Group for over twenty years now. My wife thought I had lost it when I suggested we join, but when Katrina hit, she was happy to have her bug-out bag on her back and all six of us in the van headed to her sister's house before we were called to evacuate.

My boys have all grown up knowing the importance of self-sufficiency, but also the importance of helping others. They have been at my side on multiple occasions, laying sandbags or clearing rubble, spreading awareness and even getting their friends to join. One of my proudest moments was when my son's friend, Andrew, came running up to me just to show me the fire-escape plan he'd drawn up for his family.

In all my 62 years, I've seen countless examples of how people rise up to help their fellow man, but no one can do that unless they first know how to help themselves. That's why it's essential that you soak in all the information in this book and put into practice what I teach you. By removing your own anxieties through active organization, you can be better able to support others in an emergency.

One thing you won't find in any other survival guide is that sense of togetherness that comes with a disaster. You only ever find fear-driven advice that tells you to keep to yourself and trust no one. You only ever hear about the horrible looting and hoarding that goes on and how being prepared might make you a target to be mugged or killed. In my experience, a real survival situation like we had with Katrina and Rita, and then again with Harvey, requires the mentality and conviction of heroes. If I can inspire just one more person to stop hoarding toilet paper and start preserving food properly, then I'll be satisfied. I'm not saying that a survival situation is going to be all strawberries and sunshine, but if your every interaction is going to be fear-driven, you'll be hard-pressed to work out any disputes or alliances.

So, here in this book, I will teach you how to prepare yourself, yes, but I will also challenge you to become a leader in your community. I will challenge you to be disciplined and kind unless you're left with no other choice. Regardless of what you read in Dawkins' book, our species has evolved not through our warring and self-serving ways, but through our innovation, collaboration and adaptation to hardships. As a team, you can move forward through pandemics, floods, fires, earthquakes, or whatever disaster flies your way.

Pop Quiz 1

Let's begin in this moment. Check off on this series of questions now, and then again once you've completed the book, to determine your level of readiness.

	Before	After
Do you and your family have a fire-escape plan and muster point?		
Does your escape include two possible exits from each room?		
Do you have working fire alarm(s), and extinguisher(s) on each floor of your home and do you know how to use them?		
Do you have a list of emergency numbers available for your family, which includes: fire, police, hospital, poison control and your emergency contact?		
Do you have an emergency contact outside of your area who can house you?		
Do you have region-specific plans for natural disasters? I.e. hurricanes in Louisiana, earthquakes in California, or		

tornados in Kansas?		
Does your plan involve a meeting place if family members are separated?		
Do you have reliable communication devices and extra power sources? What about a radio in case cell service is down?		
Do you know how to turn off the gas and water valves to your home in the event of a leak? Do you have the proper tools to do so?		
Do you have proper toilet and sanitation capabilities if the water was shut off?		
Do you have copies of your passports, insurance and other important paperwork in a safety deposit box or elsewhere outside the home?		
Have you rehearsed your emergency plans with your household while you were at home AND while you were separated?		
Do you have enough food to feed your household for a minimum of 72 hours?		

Do you have a supply of water, or the means to filter water for those three days?		
Would you be able to cook your food and/or boil your water without electricity or gas?		
Do you have warm clothes, extra blankets and/or a way to keep part of your house warm without electricity or gas?		
Do you have a bug-out bag with all the ten essentials and enough food and water for three days of travel?		
Do you have emergency cash on hand?		
Do you have a supply of your personal medication to last a month?		
Do you have an emergency power source for any medical/mobility devices?		
Do you have a first-aid kit with applicable supplies to your condition as well as enough supplies to support all members of your family?		

| Do you keep your vehicle's gas tank topped up? | | |

Pop Quiz 2

You have five minutes to look around your house and find one item for each of the following:

- Shelter
- Warmth
- Food
- Water
- Communication
- Illumination
- Knife/multi-tool
- First-aid kit
- Fire-starter
- Sun protection.

What you have just collected are the ten essentials, a list of items required for any stint outdoors, but also applicable to survival situations where you may have to leave your home and travel, either to an evacuation site, or to your emergency contact's home. In future chapters, I'll discuss these ten essentials in more detail. For now, congratulations on taking your first steps towards preparedness. Let's take a moment to look at how this simple exercise informs all of our emergency crews and task forces.

Chapter 1 - Lessons from the Experts

Regardless of the organization, a task force is only capable of providing relief and assistance if they know what they'll be up against. One of the problems with groups like FEMA is that under ill-prepared leadership, like we had in Katrina, they can become a detriment to the communities they're trying to serve. FEMA has always stated that there are three major events that are most likely to be devastating to America; an earthquake in California, a Hurricane in New Orleans, and an attack on New York City. Well, after 9/11, a lot of the funding for disaster relief was transferred over to Home Land Security. Suddenly one of the three possibilities was given precedence over the others. We know now the consequences of this.

A year before Katrina hit, Michael Brown, the director of FEMA, issued a training procedure known as "Hurricane Pam". It was to be a situation with 100 000 people stranded in New Orleans, and FEMA workers were to act out the scenario in order to work out the kinks. However, they lost funding for the project, and important strategies regarding medical aid, communications, and transportation were left unwritten.

We know what happens when a task force is thrown into battle without months of consistent, complex, and challenging training. Disaster. So why put ourselves and our families through that? The drills you set for your team are not meant to frighten you, they are opportunities to brainstorm and overcome possible obstacles. Let's compare two events so that you can see what I mean.

Case Study 1: Disaster in New Orleans

Apart from the horrifying winds and rains of Hurricane Katrina, another disaster loomed over the heads of people in New Orleans. Several of the parishes there were wholly unprepared for that unprecedented storm. New development into swamplands meant that 22 000 housing units were built on a flood plain, behind levees that would prove to be no match for that amount of water. Right there, is a lesson about preparedness. Not taking uncalculated risks is part of keeping ourselves and our families safe. But the promise of improved leveeing, proper building elevation, and flood insurance drew people to the area.

During the event, the city's government lacked the proper communications and mobility to evacuate the city, and in fact the officials did not even have a comprehensive plan in place to follow through with an evacuation, save to throw 15 000 people into the Superdome, which had neither the supplies to support them, nor complete protection from the winds and rain. This lack of planning meant that FEMA, the National Guard, and volunteers had their work cut out for them just playing catch up to the storm.

When the military were sent for to bring in food and water, it took them days just to get to the city because they had to clear debris from flooded roads on their way. Eventually, the refugees in the Superdome had to be shipped to another stadium in Texas. So, not only was there a lack of planning, there was a lack of supplies and communication. This is the perfect storm. This is exactly what you want to avoid, and you can avoid it by learning from history. Yes the city of New Orleans is on a much grander scale than your own planning objectives, but there are three lessons I want to repeat here,

1. A clear emergency plan needs to be in place for your team.
2. Your team must practice this plan multiple times to ferret out any problems.
3. Part of your plan needs to entail having supplies immediately available to see you through the event.

4. Part of your plan must include an escape strategy.

Case Study 2: A Calm Retreat

When my family and I moved to New Orleans in 1995, we didn't know how severe a hurricane could be on the Gulf of Mexico. It wasn't until I joined a Prepper's group that I was made aware of the possibilities. I thought the rains from Hurricane Ivan were bad enough. My participation in this group proved to be priceless because I was taught to make an emergency plan for: fires, floods, hurricanes, and pandemics. I took that information home and involved my whole family in the planning stage. Everyone knew what was expected of them, and everyone had time to think about the WORST CASE SCENARIO. Mostly, we talked about getting separated, and where we would need to meet up, but my personal favorite came from Gordon, who asked, what happens if a sea monster comes out the ocean right when the hurricane hits?

In 2005, we got to put our plan into action (sans sea monster). From August 24th to the 25th, my family and I spent the better part of the days sandbagging our property and those of our neighbors. It was hard work, and there was tension in the air, but we were committed to our task and having children running around spraying you with water guns can help ease the strain.

On the morning of August 26, my wife, Amy, and I watched the tropical storm on the television be declared a Category 2. Just as predicted, its trajectory would put it right through our neighborhood in eastern New Orleans. My wife's large eyes met mine across the breakfast table and we decided right there it was time to leave.

The boys were still on summer break then, all sleeping peacefully in their rooms. So, we called them into the kitchen. We calmly told them what was happening and that we needed to go. They were allowed to go upstairs and grab whatever book, toy or game they wanted to take with us. No one had to pack more than a backpack because we had our bug-out bags ready. Amy called her sister in Texas, who was on standby.

My wife cleaned out the fridge, my sons David and Matt somehow managed to wrangle our tom cat into his carrier, and Ben picked up our dog Ranger while Gordon collected the pets' food. I turned off our water and gas, before knocking on a few of my neighbor's doors to let them know our decision. Most of them weren't far behind us.

In about a half an hour we were packed and ready. Even with the six of us, our pets and our gear in the Dodge Caravan, we were comfortable. We didn't over-pack and most importantly, we didn't panic. It was a quiet journey out of state. We were met with open arms. It happened that we spent the better part of September with Amy's family, returning to our home only after the second storm a month later, Hurricane Rita, had subsided.

I hope this comparison has helped shine a light on those important lessons I mentioned. Moreover, I hope people realize how their own preparation truly serves the larger community. We were six fewer people that FEMA had to manage, our neighborhood had about 40 people who evacuated before the call. It makes a big difference when there are pockets of preppers out there, especially since there are many people who cannot prepare, either because they are in a care facility, or they are living on the streets, or whatever the circumstances. When you take charge of your own destiny, you free up resources for people who really need them.

In the case of Katrina, we had to get out fast. The instability of the area meant we needed to stay away. In other cases, like the recent COVID-19, staying put is the advisable decision. So let's have a look that this situation.

Case Study 3: A Country Taken Unawares

Even as I write this, Italy is leading the world's count with more than 15,000 dead from the Corona Virus (JHU, 2020). I don't want it to seem like Italy is the only country that failed to secure their people soon enough, but the fact is that their country was hit before other major centers, so at this point we have more data on them and we have a lot to learn from them.

The blame does not lay solely on the government's shoulders here. Much of the spread of the virus was attributed to the populace having a false sense of security. In many ways, people felt they would be immune and that the bug itself was not going to be the deadly thing so many alarmists thought it would be. So in that sense, a greater effort should have been made to inform and prepare citizens for the crisis and to lock down the city before it was too late. At this point, Italy is on a strict curfew with military and police patrolling the streets. However, the death toll climbs. Without going into the scary figures, why don't we consider the lessons from this situation?

1. Pay attention to the warning of experts in the field.
2. Follow the protocol not only for your sake, but for those around you.
3. Ensure you have ample supplies so you can avoid "panic-buying".

As we are finding out from this troubling time, the media does not always have the best information and neither do government officials. That is why we need to ask CDC officers (whose job it is to track infectious diseases and warn us about them) what our next actions should be AND we need to take that advice. It makes me very nervous when I see country leaders scoff at scientists and whistleblowers because here are people who have devoted their lives to a subject and we need to take them seriously. Again, I don't want to be alarmist because that isn't helpful, but I do want to highlight how my own family has coped with this event.

Case Study 4: The Virtual Family Dinner

I caught wind of Corona fairly late. On Saturday, March 14th, I was watching the news after a short hiatus from TV, and immediately this felt different from the other four "pandemics" I'd lived through since the early 2000's. Amy and I decided to cancel our weekly trip to the city the next day and instead we would live off of our frozen veg and meat and our preserves and just see how all this panned out.

I made a call to each of our sons and to my surprise, they were all well ahead of me. "Why didn't you let me know?" I was a bit irate with my boys because they'd broken a solid rule of <u>communicating with all team members</u>. I couldn't blame them though, three of them have their own families now, and Ben is in university. It can be difficult to stay in touch. Ben made the decision not to come to his "elderly" parents' house (ouch), instead he was going to bunk up with Matt's family once his school closed.

On Sunday the 15th, the news kept spilling in, our government was freeing up funds to get people tested and to support those who would be out of work. We committed to staying home and I told my work crew they'd need to take at least the next two weeks off. Luckily, I had money set aside for an event like this, so I could still pay my employees 75%

of their salaries. I wasn't sure if my insurance would cover it, so I was proactive. I know a lot of larger companies haven't been, but that to me is irresponsible.

So, since then, I've been at home with my beautiful wife keeping a virtual eye on the world. We've been self-isolated since we were first made aware of the seriousness of this situation. Last Sunday, we video-conferenced with all the boys and we ate our Sunday dinners together. That was the first time I'd ever had that experience and it sure was neat to hear my little grandkids chatting to each other through the screen. There really isn't much else to report except to say that I have taken this gift of time to finally write my book and share my experiences with you.

I'm not writing this book to give you every tool I can think of and then set you out in the wilderness. I'm writing this to help you see what your options are for your specific situation and I am shining a light on areas where you might be lacking in knowledge. It's my wish for you to continue to educate and empower yourself, always with the mentality of solution-minded planning, not fear-driven reaction.

Chapter 2 - Food

In an emergency situation, you can assume that you will either be on the move, or you will be working hard to protect your shelter and group. You may be laying sandbags, digging fire trenches, transporting supplies, or rebuilding. You can calculate your particular energy needs using the Mifflin-St. Jeor equation to find out how many calories you burn just by breathing in a 24-hour timeframe. This is your Basal Metabolic Rate (BMR).

Basal metabolic rate

IMPERIAL

Men: (4.536 × weight in pounds) + (15.88 × height in inches) − (5 × age (y)) + 5

Women: (4.536 × weight in pounds) + (15.88 × height in inches) − (5 × age (y)) − 161

METRIC

Men: (10 x weight in kg) + (6.25 x height in cm) − (5 x age (y)) + 5

Women: (10 x weight in kg) + (6.25 x height in cm) − 5 x age (y)) − 161

For example, I weigh 208 pounds, my height is 5'11" (or 71 inches), and I'm 62 years old.

As a man, I calculate: (4.536 x 208) + (15.88 x 71) − (5 x 62) + 5

= 943 + 1127 − 310 + 5

So, I burn 1765 calories a day just by being alive, not including all of the manual labour I do (I've worked as a contractor for the past 27 years). In a situation where my labour might double or triple, so will my caloric needs rise. A chart with applicable activities is shown below. It compares the energy burned in only 30 minutes for a small, medium, and large person:

Activity	125-pound person	155-pound person	185-pound person
Weight Lifting: general	90	112	133
Weight Lifting: vigorous	180	223	266

Walking: 3.5 mph	120	149	178
Hiking: cross-country	180	223	266
Orienteering	270	335	400
Gardening: general	135	167	200
Chopping & splitting wood	180	223	266
Operating heavy tools	240	298	355

Source: Harvard Medical School (Aug, 2018)

So with my BMR of 1765, and assuming it will cost me approx. 22 more calories/30 min since I'm another 30lbs heavier than the largest rating, if I carry sandbags for four hours, I'll need 1240 more calories that day, a total of 3005. Close to the classic recommended 2500/day for men or 2000/day for women, but not really. This is not including any walking, or any other chores for that day. You can do your own math for your own situation.

The point is, I recommend carrying more calorie-dense food than you expect to need, because if you are like me, you will not be able to fulfill your tasks without proper fueling. If you are like my two youngest sons, you can go hours without eating before you realize you're hungry. That's fine too, until you're starving and you realize you haven't kept track of your calorie intake/use. Always assume YOU NEED MORE THAN YOU THINK.

So take into consideration how much exercise you do day-to-day and how much energy you require regularly. Exercise often and acknowledge your hunger levels. Keep track of your eating habits because your health will suffer with any huge drop in calorie intake.

The last thing you want to do is have too little food. With your calculation in hand, now you need to think about what you are going to want to eat. I'm going to separate this into two factions: Hunkering Down and Bugging Out because they are going to have wildly different needs.

Hunkering Down

Hunkering down means staying put, possibly for a short time, possibly for the foreseeable future. In a pandemic event, or a natural disaster that does not endanger your property or your lives, staying put is recommended because you will have more variety of food, you may have a water-source and toilet nearby (if the water is not affected), and you will have shelter and hopefully warmth. Your home becomes your fortress and you need to be self-sufficient until stability and trade returns, or until you surround yourself with a cooperative community with multiple sources of food and regrowth.

Get to know your neighbors well before an event and assess their skills and their preparedness. My neighbors across the way keep chickens, the ones down the road are excellent mechanics, my wife is a nurse, and my next-door neighbor is a fine carpenter with unlimited tools and toys. Everyone you meet will have a particular skillset and you should establish connections well before disaster strikes. I suggest bringing over some preserves or baked goods. After all, food is the foundation for friendship.

So, you are going to have to hunker down for a month or more. You take a look in your pantry, what do you see? A large variety of canned, fermented, dried and baked goods and pasta of course. But what if you're celiac? Then you'll need to have a variety of options that don't involve gluten. Maybe you have some different flours that you can make your own bread, pasta and cookies with.

You check the cupboards and find all your baking needs, your spices, your jams and your peanut butter. What if you have a nut allergy? There are now seed butters out there and tahini can be sweetened too.

You check the fridge and find lots of fresh greens, condiments, some left-over chicken salad, two dozen eggs, two 2 gallon jugs of milk, and a big block of cheddar cheese.

But what if you're lactose intolerant like me? That's alright, I've tasted some different dairy replacements in my coffee and my cereal and there's nothing wrong with them (I like soy and oat the best). Plus, I have some milk alternatives that don't need to be refrigerated until they're opened, so you can save fridge space that way. I don't know if cheese is ever fully replaceable, but I don't see why you can't try those non-dairy ones in the veggie sections. They do the trick.

You check out your freezer, what's in there? A variety of vegetables, fruits, breads, buns and meats. But what if you are vegan? Well, you'll need to have replacements for those meats then and we already discussed cheese. I've seen copious amounts of faux-meats in the stores now, so that's no longer a problem for most people. If you haven't got any options near you then load up on beans, nuts, and broccoli, and consider getting yourself some essential amino acids; you can buy them in a powder form online.

The List: No matter what your specific dietary needs are, you can make it work. Let's take a look at what my wife and I have in our house so you can see what an average two-person pantry could contain.

Noodles/Pastas

___ 2 2lb boxes of Macaroni

___ 2 2lb boxes of Penne

___2 2lb boxes of Spaghetti

___ 3 ½ lb bags of Black Bean Spaghetti (GF)

___3 ½ lb bags of Mung Bean Fettuccini (GF)

___ 24 pack of Ramen Noodles

Dried Grains

___ 1 25lb bag of Jasmine Rice (GF)

___ 1 10lb bag of Basmati Rice (GF)

___ 1 12lb bag of Corn Meal (GF)

___2 5lb bags of All-Purpose Flour

___2 5lb bags of Oats

___ 1 5lb jug of Popcorn

Canned Beans/Meats

___6 cans of Tuna

___ 6 cans of Salmon

___4 cans of Hickory-Flavored Beans

___ 4 cans of Chick Peas

___2 cans of Kidney Beans (Yuck)

___ 2 cans of Black Beans

Canned Fruits/Veg

Note My wife thinks canned vegetables are disgusting, so we don't keep them, but you sure can.

___ 3 cans of Peaches

___ 2 cans of Pumpkin

___ 2 cans of Cranberry Sauce

___5 cans of Fruit Cocktail

Dried Nuts/Fruits

___ 2 4lb bags of Trail Mix

___ 1 1lb bag of Cashews

___ 1 1lb bag of Almonds

___ 2 32oz bags of Raisons

___ 1 30oz bag of Mangoes

___ 1 5lb bag of Banana Chips

Dried Meats

___ 2 1lb bags of Homemade Venison Jerky

___2 1 lb bags of Homemade Bison Jerky

Milk/Dairy/Eggs/Alternatives

___24 Local Eggs (refrigerated)

___ 1 ½ gal jug of Soy Milk (refrigerated)(V)

___ 1 ½ gal jug of Oat Milk (refrigerated)(V)

___ 5 1qt cartons of Soy Milk (V)

___ 5 1qt cartons of Oat Milk (V)

___ 1 2lb block of Cheddar

___ 1 8oz bag of Daiya Mozzarella (GF, V)

___ 2 7oz blocks of Daiya Gouda (GF, V)

___ 1 1lb tub of Margarine (GF, V)

Baking/ Cooking Supplies

___ 1 5lb bag of Sugar

___ 1 2lb bag of Brown Sugar

___ 2 8oz boxes of Baking Soda

___ 1 8oz can of Baking Powder

___ 1 2lb bag of dry yeast (frozen)

___ 1 1lb box of Salt

___ 1 1lb box of Corn Starch

___ 1 8oz bottle of Vanilla

___ 1 1lb tin of Cocoa

___ 12 cans of Coconut Milk (1 word: Curry)

___ 1 1gal tin of Olive Oil

__ 1 1gal bottle of Vegetable Oil

__ 2 1gal bottles of White Vinegar

Fresh Fruit and Veg

Note We had to have our produce delivered when COVID-19 began

__ 12 Bananas

__ 10 Apples

__ 4 Oranges

__ 1 bag of Grapes

__ 1 head of Lettuce

__ 1 bag of Spinach

__ 5 Tomatoes

__ 3 flowers of Broccoli

__ 1 head of Cauliflower

__ 2 Zucchinis

__ 2 Cucumbers

__ 4 Red/Yellow Peppers

__ 1 Purple Cabbage

__ 6 Yellow Onions

__ 2 Purple Onions

___ 1 20lb bag of Garden Red Potatoes

___ 1 5lb bag of Garden Carrots

___ 4 big Yams

___ 1 5lb box of Garden Garlic

Frozen Food

___ 10 Bison Steaks (GF)

___ 1 5lb bag of Chicken Breasts (GF)

___ 6 Locally-Fished Trout (GF)

___ 1 10lb bag of Locally-Made Pierogis (V)

___ 1 1lb bag of Peas

___ 1 1lb bag of Cauliflower, Broccoli, Carrot mix

___ 2 1lb bags of Corn

___ 2 1lb bags of Mixed Berries

___ 1 1lb bag of Blueberries

Vitamins and Minerals

___ 1 bottle (300 tabs) Multivitamin

___ 1 bottle (250 tabs) Vitamin D

___ 1 bottle (250 tabs) B Complex

___ 1 bottle (250 tabs) Iron

___ 1 bottle (250 tabs) Calcium

Condiments/Spices

___3 1lb jars of Peanut Butter

___4 16oz jars of Homemade Raspberry Jam

___ 1 16oz jar of Homemade Grape Jelly

___1 32oz bottle of Ketchup

___ 2 8oz bottles of Homemade Mustard

___ 1 12oz bottle of Relish

___ 2 ½ quart jars of Mayonnaise

___ 2 16oz bottle of Soy Sauce (GF)

___ 1 10oz bottle of each of the following: Teriyaki Sauce, Garlic Black Bean Sauce, Coconut Curry Sauce

___ 1 4oz bags of each of the following: Allspice, Basil, Bay Leaves, Black Pepper, Cajun, Cayenne, Celery Salt, Chipotle, Chives, Cinnamon, Cloves, Cumin, Dill, Fennel, (8oz) Garam Masala, Garlic Powder, Ginger, Hot Chilli Powder, Italian Spices, Jerk Seasoning, Lemon Pepper, Mustard Powder, Nutmeg, Onion Powder, Oregano, Paprika, Parsley, Poppy Seeds, Rosemary, Sage, Sea Salt, Sesame Seeds, Taco Seasoning, Yellow Curry Powder

Drinks

___4 2lb tins of Coffee (we don't mess around)

___ 1 8oz bag of each of the following loose leaf teas: Black, Chai, Chamomile, Earl Grey, Fruit mix Green, White

___ 1 5lb tin of Lemonade Powder

___ 1 5lb tin of Iced Tea Powder

There it is, our preserves in a nutshell. Keep in mind this is not including our already opened food, and the random things we try out here and there. This is just what we like to have on hand at all times. If you have a large family, then you may need to have a deep-freeze (or 2) to keep more frozen meats, fruits and vegetables, since these are the items you'll use up the most and they are the most nutrient-dense.

Without access to any groceries at all, this food would last my wife and I well over three months. We know because we have been living off this variety of foods for a long time, using it up and replacing it as we go. One thing you do not want to do is let your food go rancid because you just left it there waiting for a disaster to strike. So my tips for storing food are:

1. <u>Study how much food you consume in a week's time and what foods you regularly eat.</u> Your food storage should come straight from your actual day-to-day usage. As I mentioned, you want to be realistic about how much food you actually eat, and what kinds of foods you enjoy. Of course, you should aim to make healthy decisions; you'll notice that my wife and I

don't keep cookies and chips in the house anymore since our sons moved out, but if you have children, consider their taste buds too. It is stressful for a child to suddenly face a total absence of comfort foods, just like it is for an adult.

2. <u>Inventory your food and keep an eye on expiry dates.</u> There should be no guesswork here whatsoever. Know exactly how much you have of each item, and again, at least have an idea of how much of it you go through in a week so you can multiply that by however many months YOU want to prepare for.

3. <u>Don't buy your stores all at once, and only buy bulk where you'll use it.</u> Unless you want to be eating a whole schwack of just-expired foods in a few months, make sure you are level-headed about your shopping. If you don't bake much, then buy smaller bags of flour and boxes of baking soda, so that you don't wind up with rancid ingredients. Better yet, store opened foods in bins, tins, and jars wherever possible. If you hate oatmeal, don't buy it, buy other types of breakfast cereals but keep in mind their shelf-life and remember to rotate them out.

4. <u>Consider baking your own breads and pastries, and preserving your own vegetables, fruits, jams and meats.</u> By gaining experience in these realms, you will have a smoother transition should you suddenly have

to provide for yourself in this way. Plus, it can be fun and rewarding to make preserves and although it seems daunting, remember that in one day you can jar a lot of food. One time we had a canning party with the boys and between the four of us, (David and Matt were in university), we made over 100 preserves including canned tomatoes, beans, pickles, and trout.

One of the main reasons I can cope without a constant store of baked goods is that my wife and I bake our own. We make bread once a week and always have a stash of cookies or muffins or scones hidden away from me. If you are going to keep flour and yeast and sugar in your stores then you had better know how to use them. Getting used to making your own pastries will also save you money and make you a star among your neighbors and friends. At any potluck, mouths water for Amy's chocolate chip cookies. If I've said it once, I've said it a hundred times, no one can be your enemy when you are handing them a chocolate chip cookie.

5. <u>Grow your own food, even if it's just a mung bean plant.</u> I keep an heirloom seed bucket in the cellar at all times. I've also heard them called survival seed vaults, so you can google that. Once the seeds inside are two or three years old, I buy another bucket and I use up the old ones. Don't just "have seeds" use them!

Learn to grow your own food, not only for a survival situation, but for your own health and education. Find time and space to garden, no matter how small. Even on an apartment balcony you can buy garden bags and grow peppers, strawberries, or tomatoes. Find out what your neighbors are growing and diversify. If four people have tomato plants, grow onions or kale. Offer trades and swap gardening tips. Don't go it alone, and don't lose hope with setbacks.

I would not be satisfied if the only advice I gave you was in those few tips, so let's dig a little deeper into each section on growing, preserving, and storing foods.

Growing

Here are some easy, versatile crops to work with:

Beans and Peas: Green beans, bush beans, and any type of climbing bean/pea are ideal survival foods that don't take up much horizontal space. They offer protein, fiber, vitamins, and minerals. They grow fast and in many cases are shade-tolerant, so you don't have to devote sunny space to them. With climbing beans/peas, you need to buy or build a trellis for them. The easiest way to build one is to find two sturdy, thin branches or poles between 5' and 6' long, bury them in the ground right over your beans and use a hemp string or other cheap cord to span across them in rows two inches apart. As your beans grow, gently move their tendrils so that they climb up the trellis.

Zucchini and Cucumbers: These vegetables should be planted in the spring. They require sunlight, or shade in hot weather, and regular watering. They grow quickly and can keep growing, so even once you start harvesting, you can leave some to grow to monstrous sizes. These veggies offer fiber, potassium, and hydration.

Leafy greens: Spinach, Lettuces, Chard, Bok Choy, and Kale are all fast growing and should be planted in the spring. They can grow in containers on your window all year round, or grow in boxes in the garden. They need plenty of sun and water. Leafy greens are perfect for salads or cooked greens, and are good sources of fiber and vitamins C, A, and K. Spinach as we know contains more iron. Kale contains more calcium and it can be left in the garden over the winter.

Onions and Garlic: Like kale, garlic bulbs can be left in the garden and regrown the following spring. In many cases the second year's harvest will be larger and more plentiful than the first. Keep the bulbs moist by covering them with a 1" layer of mulch to begin with, and then a thicker, 4-5" layer for the winter months. Onions can also be planted in the fall, **only** if you live in a milder climate, otherwise, start your onions in a nursery: evenly space the seeds 1-2 inches apart and allow them to grow in your greenhouse or window for 6 weeks before transplanting into the sunny garden. This process is similar for tomato plants and other sprouts. It helps keep the plants safe, pest and weed-free, and gives them a head start.

Root Vegetables: Carrots and potatoes, yams, and sweet potatoes are essential survival foods. They contain starches which are slow burning energy sources. They contain potassium and fiber. The plants themselves are easy to grow, but require deep, aerated soil. Make space for your root veg to grow by working a pitch fork gently into the soil every now and then. For carrots, this gives them long, straight paths to follow so they don't end up being those mutant-looking things, and for potatoes, they can spread out and grow larger in the loose soil. Mulch is beneficial for your root veg, to keep them moist.

Tomatoes and Peppers: Although you will usually find people buy tomato plants, it is not difficult to start tomatoes and peppers from seed. Like the onion, you'll want to get a head start in early spring by sprouting your plants in a nursery, a sunny, well-ventilated area, and safe from frost/excessive heat/bugs/weeds. Once the plants are 3-4" high, you can transplant them to their final destination. HOWEVER: Tomatoes need time to acclimatize, arguably all plants do. Only once the outdoor temperatures are above 50°F do you want to attempt the move. You can start by finding them a partly shady spot out of the wind (the bottom shelf of a greenhouse is great) and alternating outdoors and indoors for four hours, then eight hours, until they can comfortably stay outside. Tomatoes and peppers need plenty of sun, and you need to water when the top inch of soil is dry or more often if there's a heat wave.

Gardening PRO TIPS:

- Keep your tomatoes and other finicky plants in containers (garden bags work great), so you can move them inside if a cold snap is coming.
- Keep a compost heap or a stash of organic fertilizer to give new plants a boost
- Support your tomato plants, peppers, and other vines with four 3' sticks placed around the plant, with string wrapped around them for the plant to lean on.
- A trellis is a great space saver for all vines: squash, cucumbers, etc.
- Raised beds offer protection from pests, weeds, and tree roots, and they allow you an easier bed to aerate and organize.
- You can make a natural pest-spray using various methods. Research shows that garlic is an effective agent against whiteflies and aphids (Nzanza, Nashela, 2012, Magwenya et al., 2016).

Permaculture Magazine's Garlic Spray Recipe: You use 5-6 cloves of garlic, 8 cups of water and 1 TBS of

47

castile soap. For the best results, heat the water just until it steams, add the garlic (sliced) and keep the water at that temperature for twenty minutes to release the oils from the garlic. **Don't boil**. Remove from heat and once it is cool, add the strained mixture and the soap to a spray bottle. Compost the garlic slices. You can spray your plants in the early morning or just after the hottest part of the day.

Preserving

Proper preservation of food is essential for a long shelf-life. We have already mentioned store-bought food, which you should never leave in opened bags, but instead move to jars or Mylar bags. You can dry, can or ferment your own foods and in some cases they can last years.

Drying. Moisture control is essential for all preservations, none so much as with the drying process. In many cases, you can sun-dry any sort of fruit or veg so long as they are well out of the way of mice and other vermin. You can also use an oven set at a low temperature and monitored carefully, remembering that sugar content and fat content raise the drying time for foods.

For our purposes we'll discuss sun-drying because it's free. It takes several clear, hot, breezy days for fruits and veg to dry and you need to treat them before you dry them. Vegetables will need to be blanched (that is, thrown into boiling water for 30 seconds) so that their enzymes are destroyed before they can start to decompose the plant. Light coloured fruits can be soaked in a lemon juice and water mixture at a 1:4 ratio to keep their color, though it's not necessary. Salt should be sprinkled on tomatoes to help dry them and keep them over longer periods of time.

However you treat them, make sure to chop your fruits and veg thinly enough for them to dry evenly and make sure to check on them and flip them over throughout the day and bring them in at night. If you see any animal droppings on your tray, throw out THE ENTIRE batch. If you see any signs of mold, or if water has leaked onto your racks somehow, remove the affected pieces and look over the others carefully before jarring them. In a cool, dark, DRY room, dried fruits and veg can keep for 6-12 months.

I have heard of meats like fish being sundried by First Nations people, using incredible amounts of salt, but I've never tried it and I don't see anyone recommending it. Meat can be dried in the oven, or preserved with smoking.

Smoking requires an enclosed space with proper airflow and easy access to the flame. You can achieve this by digging a two foot hole in the ground, with a mouth wide enough for your rack to lay across. Build a fire at the bottom and let it burn to a nice bed of coals. Then use only green hardwood (from deciduous trees unless you're in the tropics) to feed the fire. Softwood won't hurt you, but it will make the meat taste weird. You will need a lot of strips of hardwood tinder throughout the process, so prepare a cache before beginning.

Thinly slice whatever meat you're using and cut away the fat. **Fat spoils easily**. Salt both sides, or prepare a salty brine to marinade it in 1:16 parts salt and water. Place the slices on a metal grill, or if you have to, lay it across stripped, strong sticks and watch that they don't cook as you're working. Rotate the meat hourly to dry out both sides.

You need to keep the level of smoke consistent to prevent any flies from landing on the meat and you need the meat to be close enough to the flame for it to be cleared of bacteria, dried, but not cooked. You will know the meat is finished when it cracks if you try to bend it, if it is flexible at all, then it is not dried enough and it will collect bacteria.

Let the meat cool somewhere safe from flies and rodents and then place it in sanitized jars, or vacuum sealed bags to keep. Dried meat can be kept for up to a year. **Cooking the preserved meat before eating it is always recommended!**

Canning. The easiest way to can food is with a pressure canner, which will steam-seal the preserve for you. It's more expensive than the boiling method though, and the instructions might differ from cooker to cooker.

The boiling method: You will prepare your food first and then jar it, but there are thousands of recipes, so I'm going to keep this section brief. Before you put your prepared ingredients in the jars, make sure you've sanitized the jar AND lid by boiling them or by running them through the dishwasher on their own, at a high temperature.

You will then need:

- A wide mouthed funnel to pour ingredients into the jars.
- Jars with the two-part lids
- A chopstick/knife to remove air bubbles from your concoctions
- A vat deep enough to fully cover your jars
- A rack to fit inside the vat and keep your jars off the bottom (so they are better temperature-controlled and they don't roll around so much)
- Canning tongs to pick your cans out of the boiling water. You can't use barbecue tongs like I did because they will slip and you'll be left with smashed glass jam all over your floor.

The recipe you are using may require different boiling times, but the idea is that you'll get a suction effect on those lids just like you would have on in-store products. I'll end here by saying **practice** canning, have fun with it, and as with anything, work out the kinks before you need to.

Fermenting will require proper heat-sealing to last, but the process of fermentation is to encourage good bacteria to grow on the food in place of bad ones. You generally will be adding salt and vinegar to your vegetables before sealing them in the jar and then you'll be waiting a week at least before opening it again. Fermentation continues over time, so some foods require longer stints and some foods will turn to vinegar if left too long.

Storing

Story Time: When I first started storing food, I had a large family to care for and not a lot of space. I had the bright idea to store most of our dried foods in the laundry room because we hardly used the cupboard space there. Well the room had no ventilation and of course it was quite moist. Because I wasn't circulating out food and replacing it, and because my pastas were in bags, a lot of them went stale. My bulk candies and drink mixes, which I'd hidden away so cleverly, became mutant sugary globs. Luckily, I learned my lesson before the cans of food had more than just some surface rust on them.

Food storage is all about moisture control. Store-bought dried foods like beans and pastas have been prepared at their ideal dryness(no greater than 13% moisture). Your job is to keep the humidity around them low. In your pantry you can have a chemical dehumidifier, which is usually meant for boats or RVs. It's a cheap device and you can literally see the water it pulls out of the air because it will collect in a basin underneath the chemical package. Keep emptying that basin and keep extra refill bags handy. Ventilation is also important for moving moist air out of the pantry. Keep your door open if you don't have any pets to worry about, or at least keep it open when you're nearby, except if you are cooking! Don't let steam add moisture to your pantry.

The second lesson about storage is organization and inventory. Take stock of all that you have and make it easier for yourself by keeping your beans in one corner, your pastas in another, and so on. Don't let laziness keep you from following this rule and don't fall for the old, "ah, that should be enough". Think logically about how much food you will need, based on your earlier calculations and DIVERSIFY.

The key to food storage is to have variety. My comprehensive list of what you should have in your pantry may have seemed overwhelming but think of it this way, would you rather eat oatmeal for breakfast, soup for lunch and pasta for dinner every day for the rest of your life? Or would you like to enjoy the same variety in your diet that you do now?

Root Vegetables Storage. Unlike other preserved foods, root vegetables need a humid environment so that they do not shrivel up. A basement will do, but a cellar is better. DO NOT WASH root vegetables before storing them because this can encourage pests and the decomposition process. DO

NOT LEAVE POATOES IN THE SUNLIGHT because their enzymes begin to turn the skin toxic.

Bugging Out

Bugging out means you need to leave and leave quickly. You may not know how long you will have to be on the move, but most people can carry 3 days of food comfortably on their backs, along with the other ten essentials, which I'll expand on in Chapter 7. You should have a bug-out bag made and waiting for you at the door. Aim to have at least a 35lt backpack. If you have small children, expect to need a 40-50lt one.

The food you choose here needs to be non-perishable, lightweight and calorie/nutrient dense. No one really likes rice cakes anyway and luckily they are neither calorie-dense, nor nutrient-dense so you can leave them for the birds. You need meaty, fatty, sugary goodness. That's right, now is your opportunity to forgo the fad diets and get into the good stuff. Here are some options separated into macro-nutrients as well as vitamins and minerals.

PROTEINSTrail mix/ nuts

- Protein bars
- Dried lentils (if water is no issue)
- Jerky (there is now faux-meat jerky out there for all of you vegetarians)

CARBS
- Dried fruit
- Dried veg (for soup)
- Dried seaweed
- Squeeze pouches (apple + fruit sauce)
- Granola bars
- Chocolate, chocolate, and more chocolate (watch it doesn't melt)
- Oatmeal
- ramen/couscous/minute rice
- Freeze-dried/ready-to-eat meals

FATS
- Butter/ coconut oil (for cooking)
- Peanut butter/nut butter (good for protein too)

VITAMINS/MINERALS
- BLOCK gummies/ NUUN electrolyte mixes/salt
- multivitamin
- protein/vitamin and mineral powders

THINK VARIETY, THINK HIGH CALORIE

Do your best not to forget nutrient variety. You still need to consider all the vitamins required for a healthy lifestyle and since fresh fruit and veg will not be on the menu, consider a multivitamin, or a vitamin supplement specific to your body's needs. Are you constantly anemic?

Make sure you are eating foods high in iron. Are you at risk for osteoporosis? Cram down the calcium. Are you worried about getting enough antioxidants? Well… dried fruits and veg will have to suffice. In all these cases and more, chocolate is always going to be the answer. I'm speaking from experience when I say that you can walk for miles surviving only on chocolate chip trail mix.

Reminders for bug-out food:

1. Rotate out your foods just like you would with your regular food storage, so that nothing goes rancid.
2. Keep in mind your family's dietary needs and their taste buds when choosing foods.
3. Hydration is going to be a serious issue when you're on the move, so electrolytes are not optional.

Chapter 3 - Water

As most of you know, a human can survive three days without any water at all. But how much water do we need to drink to not only survive, but to thrive? The whole "8 cups a day" has been debunked for a while now and from the average person's experience, it makes sense. Who here has actually been able to keep that up? The more realistic rule of thumb of between 4-6 cups a day comes from Harvard Medical School (2018). However, if you are active and sweating, then you can expect to NEED MORE THAN YOU THINK. During hot months, you need to also keep in mind that drinking water is not enough, you need to have an electrolyte balance if you are sweating because you will be losing salts. A tsp of salt mixed with a touch of lemon and sugar in a cup of water is disgusting, but totally acceptable as a substitute for the fancier if not equally disgusting electrolyte mixes (most people do like them, I'm just a miserable old geezer).

Remember to drink **before** you get thirsty, because thirst is the precursor to dehydration. To avoid thirst, it's better to take smaller mouthfuls throughout the day than to chug a bunch of water all at once. Plus, chugging water can make you nauseated, especially if you are dehydrated. We can also get some of our daily water from our food or other beverages.

Consider not only the amount of water you need to drink, but also the water you will use for sanitation, laundry, and dishwashing. You may be able to get away with using grey water for laundry and sanitation so long as you have a powerful soap. I don't personally recommend using grey water for dishes, because if there was some sort of virus that you missed, it would contaminate your food.

In order to prepare for water scarcity in a **hunkering down** scenario, the simplest way is to buy and store some 5 gallon water bottles, and rotate them out so that you don't have five-year old bottles in your stores. It's not that the water itself goes bad, but plastic is plastic and eventually it will start to leech into the water. Rectangular water containers are the handiest because you can stack them on top of one another. What you need to remember is that **you cannot store water in anything other than FOOD-GRADE containers.** Don't go buying buckets just because they're cheaper. They're cheaper because they degrade. Degrading means that little particles of plastic break off and enter your drinking water. Not only that, but non-food-grade containers may house bacteria that is difficult to remove. You shouldn't even store water in containers that have held other liquids because sugars and sugar-loving bacteria are hard to remove from food-grade plastic coke bottles and milk jugs.

If water in your area is not likely to be scarce, i.e. you don't live in Nevada, California or other deserts, then your best bet might be to filter rather than store. And, again, it's great to have both options.

Now, you can buy some amazing water filters. I can't begin to describe the variety. Look for a filter that doesn't need an electric pump however, just in case the power goes out. If you don't have the money for a futuristic filter, you can build one. Bio-sand filters are used throughout third-world countries now, in order to supply people with clean drinking water even in the most impoverished places. They use a concrete basin with layers of sand and gravel to naturally clean water. There is an open-sourced manual for building a bio-sand filter, including the wooden mold into which you'll pour the concrete. You can google ohorizons.org/manuals to find the specs.

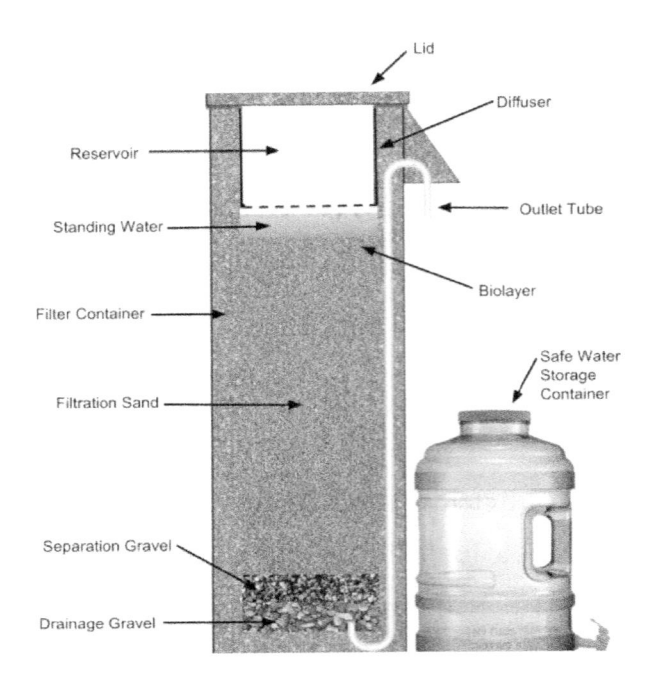

Source: ohorizons.org

To make your own, you are going to need:

- Sand, small pebbles, and larger gravel **from a quarry**
- A tall, narrow, stainless steel or opaque FOOD-GRADE container with a lid
- A plastic/metal sheet with holes in it to use as a diffuser, that can hook onto the top leaving 2" of space between it and the sand
- A flexible tube long enough to reach the bottom with still length to pour out from a hole at the top.

A possible alternative would be a blue water container with a spout at the bottom, but it would be difficult to pour the gravel into it without mixing it up, and you'll still need a mesh layer to pour water in through the top.

To sanitize your rocks and gravel before you use them, boil the two sizes separately for 1-3 minutes. WARNING: Do not plunge the boiled rocks into cold water. Allow them to cool slowly. I don't think they'll explode, but let's not risk it... Sanitize the sand by pouring boiling water over it in smaller quantities and letting it stand for five minutes, then rinse it with water to remove dust and particles. It will be finished when water runs clear.

Layering: Situate the hose so that it sits on the bottom of the container and then layer the drainage gravel on top of it. Make this layer 2" thick. The rocks should be slightly larger than blueberries.

The second layer will also be 2" thick, made of pebbles about the size of corn kernels (this layer keeps the sand from filling in the larger rocks). Make sure your hose is still stationary.

The third layer will be made of **quarry-sourced** sand and it will be between 10 to 12" thick. The thicker the better. You cannot just get sand or rocks from the pond near your house. Crushed-rock sand is cleaner and will have the proper variance of size needed for safe filtration.

Right where the water meets the sand, a bio-layer will form, that should be about 2" thick. This is the place for all the nasty little microbes to settle in and eat each other. **It takes**

30 days for this bio-layer to form, before that, your water is not guaranteed to be safe. You need an area for the microorganisms to gather, so that fewer of them pass through to the sand. Pathogens can be captured in the sand, but the bio-layer is the magic zone of this filter. It is important to keep this section wet and covered from sunlight.

Above this, you'll hang your sheet of metal or plastic with holes in it, which serves to disperse the water evenly over the sand without disturbing that bio-layer.

When **bugging out**, it is unrealistic to assume you can carry even more than a few days' supply of water on your back. So, during a bug-out situation, you need a way to clean your water of contaminants.

Chlorine Tabs

Many hikers carry good old-fashioned chlorine dioxide tablets, which will kill all bacteria, protozoa and viruses, IF given enough time. A tasty virus known as Cryptosporidium apparently takes 4 hours to remove chemically. However, different areas have different viruses to be aware of, and remember just because you are drinking from a river does not mean there is nothing to worry about, neither does the temperature of the water have anything to do with the little nasties that call it home. Aside from their benefits, chlorine tablets do not clear away debris, but you can carry coffee filters to first pour the untreated water through and then add the tablets. The chlorine taste you can mask with flavoring.

Boiling

Many people around the world right now survive by boiling their water. Boiling will kill bacteria, protozoa and viruses. However, it requires fuel, so unless you have enough fuel to boil your water and cook your food, you need to use it sparingly. If you are in an unprotected forest, you can collect wood to build a fire, and we will discuss that in a later section. There is some debate about the length of time needed to boil water for safe drinking, however the most consensual information I found stated that a rolling boil of 210°F (100°C) for 1 minute will be adequate to kill all pathogens.

If you live 3200 feet (1000 m) or more above sea level, then the cooking time increases. The most difficult pathogens to kill are viruses and since water boils at a lower temperature at higher altitudes, you need to cook those babies for 3 minutes if you want to destroy their DNA sheaths.

UV Lights

It may sound like hocus pocus, but when incoming water is passed under high-powered Ultra Violet light, the nucleic acids in any bacteria, protozoa, or viruses are destroyed and their DNA denatured. Think of getting a really bad sunburn, but you're only a single celled organism... or a bit of DNA wrapped in some protective proteins.

UV light doesn't change the water's taste, which is nice, but it requires electricity. Unless you have a store of efficient batteries and you are certain the device is high-powered enough, you may as well be blinking a flashlight at the pathogens... Another consideration is that the water needs to be absolutely clear, any debris will block the light from its intended targets, so you have to filter out debris first.

Filtration

Perhaps the best option for purifying water is a water filtration device. There are hundreds of options in terms of gravity fed filters, substrate filters, squeeze filters, and pump filters. I have used quite a variety of these and so I will give you a basic description and you can choose your own preference.

Squeeze filters/Life Straw

They can come with small flexible pouches rather than hard plastic bottles, and they'll have a filtration wand that screws into the mouth, or an external spout. In some cases a syringe will be included for back flushing your system in order to clean it after use. Though they are small, these filters can be rated for anywhere between 1 000 and 6 000 liters. The downside to these is that the micron filters are **not** small enough to root out viruses, so if you are using stagnant water, or water that is also used by animals, then you may be at risk. However, they do filter out protozoa and bacteria.

Pump filters

Just as the name suggests, these babies require a little elbow grease to get that precious H_2O pumped through. The nice thing about them is that the back flush feature is usually in their design and so you don't need a second attachment for that. Some brands are rated to remove even things as small as viruses out of water.

Gravity filters

These filters can take a longer time to filter, but they can be intense and thorough. Gravity filters will not always last longer than squeeze filters and they weigh more, but you can leave them alone to do their thing and come back for them later. Make sure you purchase one that can filter even the smallest microorganisms. You can buy a gravity filter with a carbon layer; carbon has the wonderful habit of absorbing contaminants and making the water taste better. We haven't even discussed contaminants in your water source, but filtration is the best way to remove them short of distillation. I'm not even going to go into distillation here because frankly, it's an arduous task and it removes the beneficial minerals from your water.

Buck Collins

Chapter 4 - First Aid

I have asked my lovely wife to assist me with this chapter, since she was a registered nurse for over forty years. She states that if you do not have basic training in first-aid, you should get it. <u>This book does not replace hands-on certifiable First Aid instruction and you should seek that out before offering to help someone who needs medical attention.</u> In a standard first-aid course, you will learn life-saving techniques like: how to tend large cuts, burns, sprains and broken bones, how to give CPR (there's no mouth-to-mouth these days, so don't panic), how to save someone who is choking, and how to support someone with a possible spinal injury. I cannot adequately teach this to you in a book, but I will try to at least give you an introduction through some basic scenarios.

Before we dive in, let's open up your handy dandy First Aid Kit. What's inside? Of the following list, check off what you already have and determine whether or not you need the rest, some of these items will not apply to you and some of them are just nice to have, but not vital.

___ Gloves

___ Tensor Bandage, Triangle Sling

___ Gauze

___ Medical/Sports Tape and Scissors

___ Sterile, Non-Adhesive Pads and Band Aids

___ Polysporin,

___ Emergency Blanket

___ Antibiotics

___ Pain Killers

___ Muscle Relaxants

___ Imodium

___ ASPIRIN

___ ElectrolyteTablets

___ Allergy pills/Personal Medications

___ Tweezers

___ SAM Splint

___ Pocket Face Mask (Only if you are properly trained for CPR)

___ Alcohol Swabs

___ Activated Charcoal

___ Dental Care Kit

___ Condoms/Contraceptive and Plan B Pill

___ Feminine Hygiene Products

Most of these things should be familiar to you, but I will go over a couple that may be new. Imodium and other anti-diarrheal medication can greatly reduce the effects of gastro-intestinal infections, where the person is at risk of fluid and nutrient loss from diarrhea.

A SAM Splint is a flexible aluminum brace with a stiff foam covering, used for many types of broken bones or sprains. You can keep some paracord in your first-aid kit with it, to help keep it in place around the limb.

You have probably heard all sorts of wild claims about Activated Charcoal, but I list it here solely because it can help with certain types of poisons. If you are in a survival situation and your child gets into the pain killers, you can stir 25-50 grams of activated charcoal into 4-6oz of water for them to drink. Add juice for taste if your child refuses to drink the black liquid. If they are an infant, 10-25grams, if an adult has been poisoned, anywhere between 50 and 100 grams. It's all based on weight and how much poison they've ingested, which can be hard to determine.

Activated charcoal works by binding toxins to its surface and then passing unabsorbed through the intestines. Activated charcoal is safe for everyone, even pregnant women. The side effects may be: nausea, vomiting, black stool, and a stained tongue. **WARNING**: Activated charcoal will not work with any acidic or basic poisons like sulfuric acid or bleach. It will not work for cyanide, lithium, alcohol, or formaldehyde. It also may not be successful with certain poisonous berries or plants.

Dental Emergencies and Basic Care Kit

You want to be comfortable caring for an abscess or a cracked tooth as best as you can until you can get help. Your first step is to keep your mouth clean. You can rinse it with salt (1 TBS/cup of water), or a peroxyl mouth wash (hydrogen peroxide works as well but damages your teeth and gums over prolonged use). You can buy a dental hygiene kit with a mirror and a pick to help maintain your teeth and look for problem areas and you can purchase a temporary filling replacement like Dentex in case you lose a filling or your tooth breaks and you aren't likely to see a dentist right away. You can keep cotton balls in your kit to help stop bleeding and you should always wear gloves when working on dental care.

Now, let's go over some scenarios that you are likely to face whether you are in a survival situation or not. In any medical emergency, **your first responsibility is to call the paramedics**. However, for our purposes we will assume that the emergency responders will be delayed, or will not be coming. In either case, you need to know the signs of shock and how to mitigate them.

Now **shock** doesn't mean surprised or "freaked out". It means the person's blood-pressure is so low that they are unable to get oxygenated blood to important areas of the body. The first areas to suffer are the limbs and the skin, but the organs are not far behind.

Shock can occur after any type of trauma, including, but not limited to: blunt-force trauma or blood-loss, hypothermia, hyperthermia (heat-stroke or fever), sepsis (blood-poisoning), heart-attack or stroke. You will know they are in shock because they will have cold, clammy skin that looks pale or even grey. Their lips and fingernails might appear blue from lack of oxygen. Their pulse is going to be weak, but rapid, and their breathing will be irregular. The person might be irritable, anxious, or confused, dizzy and/or fatigued. Their eyes will look hooded or faded, like they are about to pass out (because they probably are), and their pupils may be dilated. They may also feel nauseated. Before you treat a person, you need to remember the three Cs. CHECK, CALL, CARE.

Check: THE SCENE

Did you see what happened? If not, then you need to know if the area is safe to enter. Otherwise you'll become another victim, possibly with no other help on the way.

Look for fire or electric wires, fallen rock or trees, broken glass, wild animals or insects. Smell for gas or fumes, and look for a leak. Listen to what's around you. Only once you are certain there is no threat, should you approach the victim. Do you have an idea of what happened to them? Is there a low hanging branch that they brained themselves on? Are they at the bottom of a cliff, staircase, or fallen ladder?

Check: LEVEL OF CONSCIOUSNESS

Call out to the person to get their attention, clap your hands on either side of their face, and then squeeze their shoulders. DO NOT SHAKE them. You don't know if they have a spinal injury.

Check: LEVEL OF ORIENTATION

If they wake up, do they know their name? Where they are? How they got there? Ask one question at a time, and judge whether they are confused or not making sense. <u>Ask them if you can help them</u>. Ask them to stay still.

Check: ABC Airway Breathing Circulation (bleeds)

If they are speaking to you, then their airway is clear. If they are speaking to you then they are breathing, though you will need to judge if that breathing is labored, weak or irregular.

If they are unconscious, you will need to assess the ABCs on your own. With one hand on their forehead, tilt their head back to stretch the front of their throat. Use your other hand to tilt the chin up and then open their mouth. You can inspect to see if their airway is blocked, but DO NOT try to shove your fingers in their mouth to collect whatever is in there, you may force the object further down.

If you can't see anything, assess their Breathing. Keep your hands on their forehead and chin and bend your head to their mouth so you can feel and hear their breath. Face their stomach, so you can watch it rise. Count five seconds, if they have 2-3 regular breaths, you can assume that they are breathing properly. If you saw what happened and you know with certainty that NO SPINAL or CRANIAL INJURY occurred, then you can roll them into the recovery position.

If they are not breathing or if they're breathing erratically with little involuntary gasps, then you will need to call 911, call for help and begin CPR.

Otherwise, check for bleeding and broken bones by PUTTING ON GLOVES and running your hands from their head to toes. Remove outer layers of clothing carefully and be careful not to disturb their head, neck or spine as you assess them. If they are awake, you need to ask if you can help them. If they are unconscious, you need to check every inch of them, squeezing gently to find any breaks.

Broken bones will be accompanied with bruising, inflammation, sometimes deformities and misaligned bones, sometimes these will be compound fractures where the bone has pierced the skin and there will be blood.

CALL: 911

If 911 is available, you need to make that call. You can keep the person safe and administer First-Aid, but if they've gone into shock, or if they've suffered a serious injury, you will not be able to help them without proper medical training (Not what you can read here). Call 911 and stay on the line with the operator until they dismiss you, or until the rescuers arrive. Do not hang up on the dispatcher, they can be a life line during this stressful event.

If 911 is **not** available, you can call for help from your group, or call out if you are in a public space where someone might hear you. You can send that person to collect a first-aid kit, or other useful items like an AED, and you can work together to care for the person. Your best chance to help them is to stay calm and work efficiently to get them the care they need.

CARE:

Okay now let's get into some scenarios to learn specific elements of First Aid care.

Scenario 3: The Hunt

You and your 70 year old father are out hunting. As you walk through the trees, your dad keeps rolling out his arm, as if it's cramping or something. When you ask about it, he just says, "It's nothing. I slept funny." It's been a fine day and you've spent more time laughing and wandering through the woods than tracking anything. Your dad seems a bit out of breath and sometimes he has to stop walking and put a hand to his chest, like it's tight or something. You figure he's just been laughing too hard.

After a particularly raunchy joke, your father goes into a fit. He clutches his chest and falls to his knees. You ask if you can help him, but he just laughs it off. Still, you know there's something wrong here and you try to keep him still, but he just keeps saying, "It's alright. I'll be fine. Just need to get back to the hut". You decide not to let him walk back though, and you remember something you read about ASPIRIN: how

The Prepper's Survival Handbook

it is not only a pain killer, but a blood thinner, that ASPIRIN can help a person who's having a heart attack.

In your first-aid kit, you take out a dose and give it to your father, with a little sip of water. Then you lay your dad in the recovery position, on his side with his arm under his head for support and one leg bent like a kickstand. It's a chilly fall day, so you take out your emergency blanket and wrap him up so that he doesn't get too cold. You try to call 911, but you are out of range. You know you can get a signal from the hut.

Your options are:

1. Leave your father here and run to the hut.
2. Walk slowly with your dad to the hut, resting often to keep his heart rate down.
3. Stay put until your dad recovers and call for help until someone happens by.

The factors to think about in this scenario are: How much daylight is left? How popular is this trail, or how likely is it that someone is going to come by? How far away is the hut, or how long will it take you to run there and how long will your dad be alone? How will the rescue team find you, or else how will you transport your dad?

There is no wrong answer here, your actions will be specific to your situation. First, STOP, Sit down, Think about the problem, Observe the changing symptoms and environmental factors, Plan your solution. If the person is responsive, plan with them, if they are confused or unresponsive, plan *for* them.

If there is a lot of daylight left and the hut is close by, but it's unlikely that rescuers or passersby will be able to find you, maybe you choose to run to the hut and bring your quad or truck back to your father. If there is not a lot of daylight left, and your father can walk without pain or shortness of breath, maybe you go to the hut together. If you are on a popular trail, or you are with a hunting party, maybe you can stay put and call out for help.

Whatever you do, keep an eye on your father's symptoms, the ASPIRIN bought you time, but it is not a cure for a heart attack. Remember the symptoms for a heart attack are: shortness of breath, chest pain and tightness, a choking feeling and any radiating pain from the chest, neck, back or arms. WARNING: in women, heart attacks are often misdiagnosed as indigestion, because they are accompanied by stomach pain and heartburn.

Scenario 2: The Fatal Hot Dog

Your family is enjoying a BBQ with the neighbors on your campsite and all of a sudden Mrs. Stanton gives a scream, "DALE!"

When you look over, Dale is coughing and turning red. You see that there is no danger to anyone nearby, he is clearly choking. You rush over and try to calm him. You say, "Just keep coughing, you're doing great." Unfortunately, he can't get the food out and all of the sudden he stops making any noise at all. He clutches at his throat. You ask him if you can help and he nods.

PROCEDURE FOR CHOKING

If you think about what you are trying to accomplish, the J thrusts make a lot of sense and you can focus your efforts rather than just wildly trying to imitate what you've seen in a movie. Keep it in your mind, you are trying to physically dislodge an obstruction using **force** and **gravity**.

1. Instruct one of the other campers to call 911 if possible. Make sure they know the name and address of the campground and ask them to report back to you.
2. Step behind Dale and wrap your hand around his middle. Find his belly button and place your thumb just above it. If the person is too tall to allow this, help them to their knees first. If they are too wide, you'll have to help them to a table or counter and instruct them to give themselves thrusts. Pull your hands **in and up**, like a j,

moving his diaphragm upwards towards the obstruction. Give him five good thrusts.

3. Next fold the person's arms across their chest, and carefully bend them at the waist, with one hand over theirs on their chest. With the heel of your other hand, find the space right between their shoulder blades. Strike them five times here, with your hand moving towards their head. Hit them harder than you think you should, making sure that they are folded enough to let gravity help you with the action.

4. Continue your j thrusts and back strikes, five of each at a time, until the obstruction is dislodged and you hear them coughing or speaking again, OR, until they go unconscious.

Let's say Dale does go unconscious. His lips turn blue and he goes limp in your hands so you have to lower him to the ground. His wife starts screaming and running over to you, everyone is crowding in around you. Calmly ask Mrs. Stanton to sit with you and ask the others to back away. Begin CPR.

PROCEDURE FOR CPR

Again, before you rush into this, think about what you need to do. You are going to press enough force into this person to pump their heart through their sternum (the flat bone in the center of the chest). What does that look like?

You need to push into one third of the thickness of their body. Just imagine that for a moment. If the person's torso is 6 inches thick, you're going to depress the first 2 inches down, then release that again and again in rapid succession, keeping a steady beat.

Once CPR is initiated, you will not stop. You will not stop until: They regain consciousness and start pushing you away, or help arrives, or someone can relieve you, or you are exhausted.

How much energy does that take? How long will you be able to keep at it? Let's break it down.

1. With the heel of your hand, find the nipple line, or, the line that runs from their armpits to the center of their chest. Place one hand over the other, ensuring that your force is coming from the heel, not your palm or your fingers.

2. Make sure you are in a comfortable position, pad your knees if possible. Straighten your arms completely and use your body weight to add force. If you are bending your arms, you'll exhaust yourself easily and you won't be able to keep a rhythm.

3. Begin compressions. Do not stop to give breaths, unless you've been trained to do so AND you have a pocket mask. Remember, you are now the pump, keeping their blood circulating. You need to keep a rhythm of about 100 beats per minute, the rhythm of Beyonce's *Crazy in Love*, or if you are a geezer like me, the beat for the Bee Gee's song, *Staying Alive*.

After giving Dale CPR for over two minutes, you hear something rush out of his throat. You stop CPR to open his mouth and check the Airway, remembering the head tilt and chin lift. Sure enough, there is a hot dog in his mouth, rather than digging into his mouth with your fingers, you roll Dale to his side and tilt his face to the ground before attempting to remove it.

Once the hot dog is out, you roll Dale over and check his breathing. If he is not breathing, you will return to CPR. If he is breathing, call to him and try to wake him. If he doesn't wake, roll him into the recovery position and make him comfortable.

Even after a person has recovered from choking, they should seek medical help in case there is anything still lodged in the airway, or in the lungs, or if damage has been done to the esophagus.

CPR FOR CHILDREN is the same as it is for adults, but there are a couple of differences for infants. If an infant needs CPR, you will only use two fingers, still at the center of the chest, along that line from the armpits and still pushing 1/3 into their body. However, you will push slightly faster because babies have a faster heart rate, think of *It's my Life* by Bon Jovi or *Holiday* by Weezer. At present, CPR on children and infants is accompanied with breaths, but you can still save a life without them.

Using an AED

These are devices found in many public buildings, and can administer a life-saving electric charge through the victim's heart if it has even the slightest fluttering beat.

CPR can help a heart to flutter, and sometimes even to restart, but an AED can measure the electrical pulse and help to revive the patient. If there are people around who can find you an AED, it can help take the guesswork out of CPR. AED's are simple to use, but you must follow directions. To use:

1. Ensure there is no standing water under the patient. Mop it up or move the patient out of it.
2. Open up the container and find the scissors to remove all clothing from the patient's chest. If there are no scissors, use what you have. The pads must be placed on bare skin.
3. Turn on the machine.

4. Apply one pad to the right chest in line with the armpit. Apply the second pad on the left ribcage below the breast and away from the naval (There will be pictures on the pads).
5. Listen to the instructions from the device. It will tell you when you should administer a shock. When it says CLEAR: it means no one should be touching the patient.

Scenario 3: The Klutz

You are walking alone in the swamp behind your house. There was a big windstorm the day before and now there are huge trees fallen everywhere. About a half mile away from home, you see one has actually barred the path you wanted to take. You climb up onto the trunk and immediately stagger. Barely catching yourself, you decide to just walk along the trunk a little further. It's been a while since you practiced your balance. When you are halfway along the old maple, you step in a spot of moss and your foot slips right off.

You fall hard enough to hear one or both of the bones in your calf break. On the way down, you tried to grab a broken branch, but wound up slicing your hand open instead. Stunned, you take a moment to check in. Apart from the broken leg and the hand, you only detect some bruising on your tailbone. You call out for help, but you're pretty sure no one can hear you and of course, you didn't want to have your cell phone on you in nature.

The cut on your hand is deep and bleeding profusely. What's worse, there is a piece of wood sticking out of the wound and you can't move your thumb all that well.

You forgot your first aid kit at home, so what do you do? Consider it for a moment and then read on:

You take off your shirt and wrap it around the wound in your hand, cushioning the impaled piece of wood. The pain makes your wince. The pain from your leg makes you want to puke, but you look at it anyway, from the way the leg is hanging, you think both the bones are broken. You can see some discoloration and inflammation at the sight.

You pull out both of your shoestrings and you drag yourself to the edge of the trail where you break off two calf-length chunks of bark. Placing them into your sock on either side of your knee, you tie one shoe string tightly around the leg, just above the break. This is so painful that it makes you cry. Then you tie the other shoestring just below the break. That one hurts so badly that you see stars for a minute. You wish you'd worn a sweater, then at least you could have wrapped that around your leg to cushion it a bit better.

You realize that you won't have much time before your body goes into shock. So, you break a branch off the fallen tree to use as a walking stick, you grit your teeth and you get moving. Every 100 feet or so, you rest and try to call for help. You tell yourself, just get to that tree and someone will be there, just get to that rock… just get to that… house! Your small goals have led you back home and your partner is right there in the garden coming towards you. They say, "I thought I heard you call for help!"

On the car ride to the clinic, you elevate the leg and you apply ice on and off as it feels good. You keep your makeshift splint on until you get there and you don't try to remove the shirt from your hand either, in case either disturbs the wounds underneath.

DEALING with BLEEDS, BURNS and BROKEN BONES is a lot nicer when you are prepared. A Sam splint could have cradled that broken leg and kept it immobilized better than bark.

Always use gloves if you are dealing with open wounds, especially when working on another person. If you can't, then try to have the patient handle their own wounds. You can wrap gauze around a deep cut and just keep adding layers to it, do not remove anything from the wound unless you have to. It could start bleeding again. Non-adhesive pads are great for large wounds or burns because they won't get stuck to the flesh.

Do not put anything on a burn that might stick to it, otherwise the flesh will come away with that material when you go to remove it. If the skin is not broken on the burn, then you can run it under cool water for 5-10 minutes.

Scenario 4: The Feud

You and your kid are digging in the garden on a hot day. They are sullen because they had a fight with their sibling, who is moping in their room. You've been outside for a few hours and you decide to call it quits. Your child decides to stay. After you are refreshed, you go back out to check on them and right away you notice they appear dazed. They are slumped over the hoe and when you ask what's wrong, they say, "Nothing, I've just got a headache."

<u>You offer them a drink of water and ask them to come out of the heat.</u>They take one look up at the house, see their sibling sticking their tongue out at them, and refuse to go inside. You approach and put your hand on their forehead. They are quite hot and their cheeks are flushed. They push you away, bent on their work. You can see sweat stains all down their shirt, but still they say they won't stop until the garden is finished.

<u>Insisting that they at least get to the shade, you promise to bring them a sweet drink</u>. However, none of your coercing works. You try to grab their hand and physically bring them out of the sweltering heat. Your child's speech is now confused, they are lashing out angrily and they look like they might puke. They are suddenly pale and when you touch

them again, their skin is bone dry. You scoop the child up now that they are losing strength and you head into the house. You remove any constricting clothing, and place the child in the recovery position. Call 911 if available and then call your other child to get some wet towels to drape over their body. Turn on a fan full blast, or physically fan them with a damp cloth.

Hyperthermia doesn't happen as fast as this, but it can still surprise you, especially if you are distracted, or working. Luckily, our bodies go through stages and so there are signs along the way that we must pay attention to. The temperature, colour and feel of the skin will be the biggest indicators. Hot, sweaty, flushed skin means the person is at risk and needs to find shade and drink fluid; water with electrolytes is best. Hot, pale, dry skin means the person is in heat-stroke and will possibly go into shock, or worse, have a seizure. Do not offer fluids or food to someone who is in shock or is unresponsive. Cool them down and keep them in the recovery position. Keep an eye on their symptoms.

Hypothermia occurs with a similar degradation. First the person will shiver, they will have cold or numb extremities and they may feel weak or drowsy. Then their breathing might slow and their pulse will grow weak. Similar to hyperthermia, the person may become confused or dizzy and their speech may be slurred or fumbled. They may paradoxically start to remove clothing, at which point you should be very concerned. Once they are reaching hypothermia they will stop shivering altogether, and their blood pressure will be so low that they may lose consciousness.

Your job is to take action long before this scary ending. If someone is shivering and complaining of serious cold, they need to get out of the elements and warm up. If they are past that point and their pulse is weak and they fade in and out of consciousness, then you need to immediately make camp, light a fire and warm them up.

The process of thawing them out needs to be slow, though. If you heat someone up too fast, especially if they have frostbite, you will cause even further complications. Remove any wet clothes and put them in warm ones, use your own body heat to warm them if you can, and don't offer them anything to eat or drink unless they are fully conscious. If they are conscious, then digestion can help to heat them up from the inside. In children and the elderly, extreme temperatures are more serious.When you are in the elements, be aware of changes to yourself or your group and don't discount any abnormalities in behavior or appearance.

Scenario 5: Out of the blue

You are out collecting wood with your good friend, enjoying the cool autumn air. You have felled two trees, and are in the process of sawing them into smaller pieces, when your partner goes quiet. It's strange because they were so chatty on the way into the woods and during your time here. When you ask them what's wrong, all they can say is that they feel funny. You ask if they are nauseated and they say, "kind of". You ask if their head is hurting and they say, "On and off". You decide to take a break.

You sit them down on a log and it's a good thing you do because just then, their entire body seizes up and they go into a spasm like you've never seen before. You try to guide them to the ground so they don't bust their head, but as soon as they're down, you get out of the way. You use all your strength to move the log over so that they don't smash their head against it. You call out for help in case there's anyone in the woods nearby. The seizure could have lasted 20 seconds, or it could have been 2 minutes; either way, you just know that it was a bad one. There's red foam at the corner of their mouth. You wait a short time before approaching, just in case they start up again, but when you're sure they are finished, you try to wake them by calling their name and clapping your hands. They are groggy and annoyed with you. They don't want to be touched and they get seriously angry when you ask if you can help them.

You stay back and wait for them to come around. They touch their tongue with their fingers and see that they've bitten it, blood is reddening their mouth. They look down and see that they lost control of their bladder, you offer your sweater for them to wrap around. They look to you for answers now and you explain that they had a seizure. They seem uncertain and when you ask if this has happened before, they nod. You ask if they have epilepsy and they say no, but their father does. The two of you decide to wait a few more minutes until they are okay to walk and then you head back to your truck to drive to the hospital.

If the hospital was not an option, you'd need to find some medical advice. They probably need to begin a regiment of anti-seizure medication. Likely, they need some imaging taken of their brain as well. Epilepsy is a life-long illness, but with proper treatment, it doesn't always have to impact their life.

These scenarios are only a glimpse of what can go wrong when there's no one around to help. Getting trained in first-aid will prepare you further to help yourself and your loved ones in a difficult time. I hope you recognize at least that depending on the emergency, there are always going to be ways to mitigate damage while you await help, or while you transport the person. The main things you'll want to remember are:

1. Calm yourself. Do not cause more damage by rushing into action. Assess the scene, assess the person's ABC's, CALL 911 if possible and only then care for the injuries you see.

2. Protect the head, neck and spine at all times and DO NOT MOVE the person if you suspect an injury. Transporting people with spinal injuries is beyond the scope of this book.
3. Administer CPR immediately after you've called for help if the person is Unconscious and NOT BREATHING.
4. Cover and wrap any bleeds, applying pressure to the wound.
5. Immobilize any broken bones with tensor bandage, slings, or splints.
6. DO NOT REMOVE any impaled objects, immobilize them in the body with gauze padding and tape until you can find medical care.

Chapter 5 - Children

A major part of parenting is planning. Any parent of three or more kids knows that without a game plan, family outings become free-for-alls, and group activities can become flat out brawls. Planning also means getting geared up for anything. Your supplies will depend on the ages of your children, but if they are infants or toddlers, do you have a range of diapers for them? The world may be stalled, but they are still going to grow. Keep either adjustable, washable cloth diapers, or the next couple of sizes for them to grow into. Do you have enough formula or baby food? Do you have a means of making food if you run out? A blender and a stash of vegetables can be a saving grace in that crucial weaning period.

Are your children's vaccinations up to date and are yours? Now don't give me any guff about not trusting vaccinations. I'm writing to you from the middle of a pandemic, one of hundreds that this species has faced and one that we will conquer too, only once we've created an immune-defence against it. You want to weigh the possible side-effects of vaccinations against diseases like polio? Typhoid? Tetanus?

Make a check list of the things you use on a day to day basis and decide how much you would need for at least over a month.___ Diapers, Wipes, Change Pads, Cream

___ Clothes to grow into, Seasonal Outerwear

___ Bottles, Sippy Cups, Formula/Food

___ Quality Shoes and Boots

___ Baby Thermometer, Cold/Fever Medicine

___ Baby Carrier/ Stroller

___ Toys and Books

___ Cloths and Towels

If your child is not old enough to understand what's happening, what are you going to tell them? In an emergency, you need to keep children in the loop on what is happening so that they know what is expected of them and so they can help wherever they can. The last thing you want to do is panic a child, but you also don't need to keep everything from them. That would be irresponsible and it will only mean you have to keep up a ruse until the situation is over. Speak calmly to them, without too many details and set them with simple tasks to follow.

Children want to help. They want to be a part of the action. Give your children tasks that match their temperament and strength and always try to add fun to the work. I already mentioned how my boys were keeping us cool as we laid sandbags, there's no reason why your children can't get involved in the work so long as they are kept safe. What is more, you want your children where you can see them and you want to give them work that they will enjoy. Meaningful work is the greatest gift you can give your child because it teaches them life skills, it helps them to feel important and confident in themselves and it will take their mind off of other things, especially during hard times.

Of course, during something like a pandemic, there isn't always work to be done, and still kids need some way to entertain themselves. When my family and I had to bug-out during Katrina, we didn't end up needing much of the survival items that were in our bug-out bags, but my wife had the smart idea to pack activity books for the drive and of course our sons had a couple of Gameboys and some books. It is always going to be worth the extra weight to have at least some small tokens of amusement. Handheld games have given way to cellphones, which can be expensive, but they have thousands of games and they have the added security of always knowing where your teenagers are, whether you want to or not.

Being on the move with kids is easy, there is always something to explore and always something to do. If you need to camp out with the kids, you can keep them busy for hours just gathering firewood or searching for bugs.

If you are trapped in a house with your children, on the other hand, it can be a real test of patience. We know that children can wear our nerves thin, that is why you must insist on order and work of some sort, to give them purpose and set a pace for the household. Older children can be given lessons to complete, younger children can be given art and science activities. Remember your child will always find some way to occupy themselves, your job is to negotiate how much time they can spend playing games and watching movies so that they don't lose the structure that is so vital for a healthy childhood.

Education is going to be a puzzle as well. Some schools will offer off-campus tasks, others may not. Whenever possible, complete educational activities *with* your children so you can guide and encourage them, gauge their strengths and keep an eye on the things they struggle with. It was during Katrina that we finally realized our eldest had dyslexia. We were listening to him trying to read to his siblings and my wife and I caught on to his disability. In a way, the hurricane was a blessing because it gave us time to get ahead with him.

He was 15, just starting high school and secretly feeling anxious and stupid. I had always just assumed he hated reading, I didn't think he was really struggling with it. My wife spent that month coaching him through phonics lessons and he wound up going back to school feeling brighter than before. One on one learning can be challenging though. Your children are going to test you. Remain stern, but not unyielding. Remain focused but not blind to their needs. They can't spend all day learning just as they can't spend all day on the computer. The effort you put into your children is never a waste, no matter the burden on your nerves.

Here are some tips for being at home with the kids:

1. <u>Set a routine and stick to it</u>. As much as possible, lay out your schedule for each day so that your children know what to expect, and what is expected of them. Allow down time and free play of course, but have it all written out in an easy-to-read schedule. If they are mature enough, allow them to make the schedule with you. Explain why routine is important: it helps us concentrate on important tasks, it keeps us from feeling bored or forgetting what to do, it gives us a sense of accomplishment, and it means that we always know what's coming next.

2. <u>Make sure you break up the day with physical exercise and if possible, outdoor play</u>. Kids need

fresh air whether they like it or not. They also need movement. Our boys were always active, but not all kids are. Don't feel like you have to force your kids to play hockey, but at least find something they enjoy that gets them moving and if nothing does, then find some garden work or a nice trail to walk together, anything to get their heart beating and to get a chance to have unstructured fun together.

3. **Take care of yourself**. Stay in contact with your support network, of grandparents, other parents, and friends. Take time for yourself whenever you can. Raising children is not for wimps. You may be more tired than you've ever been in your life and you may be at your wits end somedays. In my childhood, parents resorted to spanking children and locking them away when they were unmanageable, and that is an easy rut to fall into. You need to make sure you have someone to vent to, so you don't take frustrations out on your children. <u>When talking about your issues, make sure to focus on solutions, rather than problems, or else when you go back to your kids, your frustration will only be compounded.</u>

4. <u>The internet is your greatest resource</u>. What can't we teach our children now that we have access to

the World Wide Web? Don't feel like you have to come up with thirty days of activities, use online materials and lessons to teach and engage your kids. Call up the grandparents on FaceTime, have online playdates with other children. Find online games that are both fun and educational.

5. <u>Stay in the moment.</u> It's really easy to worry about what's going to happen to our family and it's really easy to despair. Whenever you naturally remember to do so, just breathe in and be right where you are, holding down a toddler as you try to slap a diaper on them, or trying to coerce a teenager out of their room. Right where you are, that's where you need to be. You are a rock to your family and your love is enough.

Chapter 6 - Day-to-Day Needs

Until now, I have only really hinted at the ten essentials, but I'd like to open those up in more detail in this chapter. Anyone who has camped or backpacked in the wilderness has a keen understanding of what is and is not essential for daily life. Heck, some hard-core dirt bags might think my list is even too ritzy. The way I see it, we can use the backcountry man's ten essentials to root out what exactly should go into your Bug-Out Bag and what you should make sure to stock your house with.

I've discussed the first three needs in detail; food, water, and a first-aid kit for emergencies. Next, we have shelter, warmth, fire, illumination, knife/tools, navigation, and sun protection. You have some options here in terms of how you pack your personal bug-out bag, but obviously you want to pack light in case you have to walk, and you want to buy quality materials so that you don't have to worry about a leaky tent or a broken headlamp. Still it is important to always have a sewing kit with strong thread and safety pins for your backpack and clothing, and a repair kit for your tent/tarps. And again, you also want to keep in consideration what needs your children have.

Shelter: For a shelter, you have to keep in mind the size of your family and the level of comfort you want to maintain. My wife and I both carried a light-weight three-man tent when we had the kids, and we made sure to have a cold-weather sleeping bag and a foam sleeping roll in each kid's backpack and our own. We had a tent patch kit and some extra duct tape in my bag as well. We also carried four emergency blankets in case we needed immediate cover. These are extremely compact and really only for emergencies, but they can keep a child warm if they are separated from you, so we put one in each boy's bag and taught them the importance of these "space blankets" early on.

Warmth: Along with shelter, you need to be able to stay warm if you are moving through colder months. Extra clothes, puffy jackets and raincoats/pants winter coats/pants may be packed seasonally. Always remember that cotton is a dangerous fabric to wear since it absorbs water and stays cool, so you can put yourself at risk of hypothermia if you only rely on cotton. Wool is the best, at least for the base layer. Layering your clothes will help you regulate your temperature. Keep a thin, breathable base layer, a warm, puffy or fleece mid-layer, and a rainproof outer layer.Also keep a beanie and warm gloves. Whenever possible, try not to sweat into your clothes, and always keep dry socks and shoes. Not only will cold feet contribute to a loss in overall body heat, but wet feet are prone to blisters. Wool or synthetic socks are non-negotiable. Do not wear cotton socks.

Fire: Waterproof matches, a heavy-duty lighter, or a simple flint stick can all be lifesaving when you need to make camp and keep warm. To start a fire, clear a small circle of any forest debris and line it with stones. This protects the area around it from burning. Begin with tinder, the smallest and lightest form of kindling, made up of thin strips of wood, lichen, leaves, newspaper, or if you're creative, toilet paper rolls filled with dryer lint. Make a small pile of tinder in the center of your fire and then build a small teepee of kindling around it, leaving plenty of spaces for air to move through. The kindling will be made of thicker strips of wood and sticks, about the width of your pinky finger. It's best to have a good cache of kindling because you'll need fair amount to get the fire warm enough to burn larger pieces of wood. Always use dry wood where possible and again, have a good stash of wood prepared so that you don't have to go wandering out in the dark later. Fire is a tool for cooking, a source of warmth, and of course, it is a source of comfort for weary travellers.

Illumination is pretty straight-forward. A headlamp is the best because you can keep your hands free, but you should check it before a journey and always carry spare batteries. A wind-up flashlight is an ok trade off because you don't need batteries.

Carrying a **Knife** or Multi-tool is essential because you can use that to cut rope, dig up roots, cut up food, or shape wood for building. A saw with a serrated edge is arguably faster for cutting firewood though, and you can buy one with a folding edge. Knives are not generally the tool of choice if you expect to need to hunt while you're bugging out. You could however duct tape your knife to a sturdy stick and create a spear for wild turkey or possibly rabbits. You ought to consider a bow or a rifle if you're serious about hunting. Along the same lines, you should have an animal repellant. I suggest Bear Spray over a Bear Banger because there's less chance of you blowing off your own skin.

Navigation: You do not want to get lost in the woods on your way to safety. If you are leaving your house, have a destination and know your path to get there. Use a map and compass if you know how, or else make sure you have a reliable gps or app on your phone and a means to keep your device charged. There are solar panels out there that hook directly into USB ports.

Sun Protection: Avoid hyperthermia by wearing a baseball cap or better yet, a full sun hat. Use sunscreen if you're going to be out in the sun. Seek out shade when you're outside for many hours and always stay hydrated.

If you do not need to leave your home, you will have basically the same needs for: food, water, first-aid, shelter, warmth, illumination, tools, and sun protection. Navigation and fire are less crucial depending on your circumstance. If you're at home, you have different needs too, you may not be on the move, so you'll need:

Entertainment: Staying put means you'll have access to many of the creature comforts you have these days. It may be wise to invest in some non-electrical toys and activities like board games, books, and hobby materials (sewing, crafts, sports, music etc.).If you have children then the need for entertainment and education increases. You can find science and art kits, along with all kinds of activity books for math, social, science and English. On the move, you should at least have a pack of cards and maybe some of those light-weight games like small chess/checkers boards, colouring books and markers, puzzles, a trivia book or book of scary stories etc. Entertainment comes into play not for idle amusement, but for sanity and wellbeing, which we will discuss in chapter 9.

Personal Hygiene:

Here's a thought experiment, you plan to spend a week volunteering to build a school in Northern Africa. There will be no running water where you're staying and no more than a hole in the ground for a toilet. What toiletries will you bring? Keep in mind that you won't recognize any brands when you land and pretend that airport security would let you past with more than 3.4oz of fluids...

_____
_____
_____
_____

What on that list is a luxury? What is a necessity?

I find we always need fewer items for cleanliness than we expect. When we know we are going to be hard at work building, gardening, chopping wood, or hunting and foraging, we tend to focus less on our appearance than if we were going into the office or a restaurant. That being said, my grandfather always taught me that being clean and well-kempt is not for pride or ego, it's for stability and purpose. If you stay in your pajamas all day, you have that tinge to the day, that sense of freedom, sure, but also of unconcern. The same goes for improper bathing, you will feel just as gross as you are and be less willing to carry out your daily tasks.

Your everyday routine is not going to be the same if you lack water or if you are in isolation. It's easy to neglect cleanliness when everyone around us is just as dirty and there's no one but our friends and family to see. Still, you do not want to fall into habits like not bathing, not brushing your teeth, or not caring for your hair and nails. Trillions of microbes are on your skin right now, just waiting for you to neglect to cleanse so that they can wriggle their way in. Pimples can turn into open sores, ingrown hairs can become staph infections, long beautiful hair will dread up and your nails will become cesspools for bacteria.

It's not that you need to have every tincture on the shelf, heck, I'm the kind of person who could care less how soft my hair is. I prefer to use Dr. Bronner's castile soap for literally everything. It serves as body wash, shampoo, hand soap, and dish soap. If that's not your style, you can try to find gallon jugs of your preferred soaps and shampoos and travel sizes for your bug-out bag.

Now back in the days of aristocracy and no running water, the rich wore all sorts of flowery perfumes to hide the stink on their skin. They would have paid big bucks to have a stick of deodorant. You can buy deodorant in bulk at Costco, or at least have one extra lying around in case you need it.

For razors, I have a secret. More blades ≠ better shave. More blades = more waste + less space. I've always used a safety razor because I save a lot of money being a man who shaves every day. My wife caught on to this early in our marriage. She stopped buying those ridiculous, clunky $20 contraptions catered to women and bought her own safety razor. Instead of having a thousand razors stashed somewhere in your house, have a single stainless steel razor and a thousand blades (if you must).

If you are a person who feels like make-up is important to your wellbeing, find out why and find out what you can change to feel okay without it. If you need a manicure every week and a new hairstyle every month, search either for alternatives to these luxuries, or search inside for something that gives you the same feeling without the constant maintenance and cost. My partner informed me that this is not good advice for women who are accustomed to these treatments, but I asked her if she knew any salons that meant to stay open during COVID-19 or during the next Hurricane.

Cleaning:

Thought experiment: If you only had enough money to buy one cleaning ingredient for your whole house, what would you choose?

There are hundreds of brands of cleaners that are perfect for all surfaces. We lie to ourselves thinking we need this product for the kitchen, that one for the bathroom. Myself, I'd take good old bleach before I'd spend more money on fancy cleaners, but keep in mind I don't have a sensitive nose and I always use gloves. Some people just can't handle the stuff and that's fine. However, even when diluted with water at a ratio of 1:10, bleach denatures the proteins of microbes and thus can kill everything. Plus, it's cheaper than cheap.

Without power or water, you will rely heavily on cleaning supplies to stave off microbes. Think of having a stock of your particular detergents and household cleaners that could last you more than a few months. Buying these things in bulk is generally going to save you time and money. I'll give you a peak into our laundry room to see what sort of products we keep.

__ 2 1gal jugs of Bleach

__ 1 1 gal jug of Dr. Bronner's Castile Soap

__ 2 1.5gal tins of Comet Cleaner (dry bleach)

__ 2 1gal jugs of Laundry Detergent

__ 2 1gal jugs of Dish Detergent

__ 2 pairs of Rubber Gloves

__ 1.2 million sponges

__ Ditto steel wool pads and rags there are definitely items here that we could do without and for some people there are items that seem to be missing. There are also special considerations to keep in mind:

- If you are without power, how will you vacuum your floors, or at least, how will you avoid dirtying your carpet? Keep a broom, a scrub brush and a stain remover.
- How will you scrub the kitchen or the floors if there's no running water? Make sure you have a mop bucket and a water source.
- And how will you use the toilet? Generally speaking, toilets will still flush so long as you have water to pour into the tank. If you are on a septic system that uses electricity to power the pump, what is your back up option? You could hook up an emergency generator or solar panel to keep it running.
- In an apartment building, the need to haul water and store water may arise, so do you have the means to do that? What sort of pulley system could you and your neighbors envision?

Other problems may arise depending on your circumstances, so think about it. Actually envision a day, a week, or a month without power or water. Could you do it? If the answer is no, then you ought to consider making some changes so that you could live comfortably should that disaster strike. Remember, the solution isn't always staying put, if you have a family member out of state who could house you, that's an option. If you have a friend who's off grid and could keep you, you could go there too.

Maintenance:

I think it's Murphy's Law that says whatever the worst thing is that could happen, will happen. It's important to be ready for a leaky roof, or a broken window right when you least suspect it. I am a huge proponent for having your own set of basic tools including, but not limited to:

___ A Hammer and various sizes of Nails

___ A Drill with various Bits and lengths of screws

___ A Screwdriver with various heads

___ A Handsaw

___ An Extension Cord (30-50ft)

___ AnAdjustable Wrench

___ Pliers

___ A Sewing Kit with safety pins, and strong threads

___ Needle-Nosed Pliers

___ Exacto-Knife

___ Duct Tape

___ Tarps and plastic sheets

___ Bungee Cords and zip ties

___ A Ladder

___ Wood Glue and Crazy Glue (and shoe glue if you're as cheap as I am)

___ An Axe and Whetstone (with oil for sharpening)

___ Safety Goggles and thick Work Gloves

___ A Level and Stud Finder

___ Heavy-duty bags

___ WD 40 (not just for lubrication, can also repel wasps and other insects from building nests, and clean grease and dirt off of carpets, floors, and hands)

___ Paracord (comes in handy for keeping your life together)

___ A Sewing Kit with strong thread and safety pins

___ Fishing Tackle

___ Gardening tools like: a spade, a rake, a hoe, gloves, soil, seeds, twine and wood for a trellis, chicken wire to keep out animals   Regardless of if you ever need to board up a window or fix a roof, you will use these tools regularly. Having tools will afford you the freedom to build and fix furniture and items around your home, instead of having to throw things away and buy anew. Look around at your different vehicles, devices and constructions and determine what types of tools you'd need to fix them. You may need a specific drill bit, or a special part and it is important to have those on hand. If you are adept with power tools, I might suggest a few other items, but again, it's difficult without power. A chainsaw does come in handy for felling trees and cutting them into firewood. Plus it runs on gasoline...

The point is, there is more to your day than food and water. How will you fill your time? What hiccups are you going to meet along the way and how will you overcome them? Only you can truly prepare for your day-to-day needs, but you should be proactive and seek out solutions to problems like: clogged drains/toilets, broken furniture or appliances, rodents or pests, seasonal storms or snowfall. Sometimes the answer to your struggles is not going out and buying a new toy, but borrowing from your carpenter neighbor and trading him some canned peaches in return.

Special Considerations for People with Disabilities:

If you or your loved ones have specific needs based on a disability or illness, you are going to want to make life comfortable for yourselves by tending to those needs thoroughly. Your family's situation is going to be unique, of course, so you already know what you will need on a day-to-day basis. That being said, here are some general suggestions that may be new for you:

For illness, or incapacitation:

- Make sure you will have adequate medication for at least a month with the proper refrigeration/storage. This may include sharps

and IVs, pill organizers, inhalers, epi-pens and/or blood sugar tests. If you are on oxygen, you need to have extra tanks too.
- You may need a supply of toileting products such as: catheter bags/diapers, a bed pan, cloths, sponges, sheets and cleaning products.
- Any sort of electric life-support device will also require a back-up power source.
- Caregivers need to pack a bug-out bag with or for the ill or elderly person, to ensure nothing is forgotten. Be sure to have medications and daily-use items in an easy to grab place. You can pre-pack toileting and cleaning needs, toothbrush and grooming items, food and water, along with warm clothes, outerwear and good shoes. It is unlikely that the person will be comfortable camping, so have an escape plan that involves a warm bed at night.

For mobility needs:
- A mobility device like a cane, walker, scooter, or wheelchair and if it's a motorized chair, you'll need a spare battery and a means to charge it. There are solar generators available these days that can charge large capacity batteries. In some cases, chairs and scooters can be modified to better handle a bug-out

situation. Add all-terrain tires, a powerful front light, and a rain cover to feel more confident should you need to take any dirt roads.

- If your condition may worsen over time, do you have the next device available? For example if you rely heavily on your walker, you might want to have a scooter or chair in case you need more support in the weeks to come.

- Make sure you have adequate lighting, guard rails, slip-grips on stairs/ramps, and a clean living space. Falls are a leading cause of injury and you want to avoid them by keeping your space safe.

- For a bug-out bag, you may need something modified to be easier to carry, or something on wheels. If you need a means of transportation and assistance, make that arrangement. You don't want to have to stress about getting out of the house. It's always better to have a coordinated plan in place. You also want to pack a high-powered headlamp, and possibly a portable urinal so that you don't have to make trips in the dark. Plus they just come in handy when you're on the move.

For the Visually Impaired AND those with glasses:

- If you wear glasses, keep a repair kit and a second pair of glasses if you can
- If you wear contacts, have a month's supply, but keep glasses as well
- If you have a service animal, you'll need to have adequate food for them. You'll also need to keep them up-to-date with their shots and vet checks.
- For yourself, if you are partially blind, you'll need to take the same precautions with lighting, grips and guides around the house to prevent falls. If your vision is expected to decay, plan for that by making your home accessible and memorisable.
- Pack with help, a bug-out bag that does not impede your movement too much. Plan a route that you know. More importantly, practice getting to your designated spot from the house many times, so that you have the muscle memory. Consider having transportation for if there is a disaster so that you can focus on staying secure rather than focusing on how you'd get out.
- Pay attention to reports so that you are in the loop about any early evacuations. You'll want to be ahead of the crowd.

For the Hearing Impaired:

- Have a special vibrating alert on your phone to tell you of incoming storms, have vibrating fire alarms and carbon monoxide alarms too.
- Make sure you have a means of communicating with your family and friends in-person and online, but also carry a means to communicate with strangers.
- Ensure you have a means of charging all hearing aids and of course, your phone.

Developmental/ Sensory Challenges:

If your loved one has a delay of any kind, you'll need to be keenly aware of their comfort zone. What can you tell them to keep them calm? What can you provide for them to make sure they feel safe and secure? There are many tools for those who don't like bright lights and loud noises, like dark lenses and earphones. There are thunder blankets for those who need to feel more sheltered. Each condition is going to come with its own challenges, but you know from everyday experience what your loved one needs. Here are some considerations:

- Toileting and sanitary products, grooming products
- Specialized devices for sensory/mobility issues and a power source
- Any medications they require and a means to store them
- A bug-out bag that you can carry if they cannot
- An escape plan that is uncomplicated that you can practice with them multiple times until they are comfortable with the process and you've smoothed out all the kinks. It's important for everyone to know the drill because sudden changes or expectations can make a person anxious or worse, terrified.

Chapter 7 - Mental Health Emergency Kit

The fear of having our entire life flipped upside down can be overwhelming for most people. It is safe to say that even the planning process can bring up a lot of fear and emotion for people. Sometimes in our planning, we become misguided to think that every storm or bug is going to be "The One" and that can cause us to revert to primal behaviors of hording and suspicion. That is why I want you to read this chapter as many times as you can to remind yourself of your purpose in all of this. First a couple of questions,

1. What are some of the worries and fears you have about emergencies?

   _____
   _____
   _____
   _____
   _____

_____
_____
_____
_____

_____

Possible answers: that I won't be able to make it, that I will face unemployment, or poverty, that I won't be able to keep my family safe and fed, that I will lose hope

2. For each fear you named, what are two solutions you can come up with to combat this should it come to fruition?

_____
_____
_____
_____
_____
_____
_____
_____
_____

_____

Possible answers: I can reach out to friends and family for support, I can find work and sanctuary in other areas, I can save up an emergency fund, I can seek refuge with government programs, non-profit aid or churches, I can remember that I have a purpose and I can move towards that no matter what I'm faced with.

3. Who can you turn to for support?

   _____
   _____
   _____
   _____
   _____
   _____

4. Who depends on you?

   _____
   _____
   _____
   _____
   _____
   _____

5. Do you have access to professional help for any extreme changes in behavior or mood that you find unmanageable?

   Yes ☐ No ☐

6. If you answered no, what steps can you take to make sure you have that access should your need arise? (You don't have to seek help, but you do need to know where to go if you need it).

7. What emotions are you prone to when under stress and how do they affect your thinking?

Possible answers: anger and anxiety. They make me think negatively and they cause me to focus on the worst-case scenario and the worst parts of a situation

8. When these emotions come up, what can you do to help yourself?

Buck Collins

_____
_____
_____
_____
_____
_____
_____

_____

Possible answer: I can rest with the anger and the anxiety, without trying to push them away, but without indulging them either. I can just see my emotions for what they are and I can work through them because I know that they are a part of my personality, but they don't have to define me or incapacitate me.

9. What trains of thought are you prone to under stress and how do they affect your emotions?

_____
_____
_____
_____
_____
_____
_____
_____

_____

Possible answer: I am prone to following the negative scenarios all the way to the bitter end.

10. When these thoughts come up, what can you do to help yourself?

_____
_____
_____
_____
_____
_____
_____
_____
_____

Possible answer: I can accept that my thoughts are my coping mechanism and just because I have negative thoughts does not make me a negative person. I can still be capable and clear-headed even when I'm in the middle of a scary thought, and even when I've blown things out of proportion in my mind.

Prepping is a means to steady the mind. You want to remove any and all hysterics from the operations of storing food, readying escape plans, and creating a self-sufficient space. You should feel more at ease with every action, not less. If you find that the news reports are making your heart rate jump and your thoughts speed madly in all directions, turn

them off. You are not ignoring the real threat that may be out there, you are taking a break from it to re-center yourself. One thing I've noticed about myself these last few weeks is that I can't help but watch every report and read every article I can on the situation. I just have to know what's next and how can I be ready. While this isn't inherentlya bad thing, it has become an obsession for me. I can see how my focus is blurred when I see all the politics and hearsay surrounding this pandemic and it sometimes keeps me from sleeping at night.

Possibly the worst thing we can do for ourselves is run our bodies and minds into the ground by trying to see every possible threat that might be coming our way. Your mental health demands that you are committed to staying fit, staying healthy, and most importantly, staying relaxed regardless of what appears on your computer screen.

Many people wrongfully associate relaxation with laziness. You can be fully relaxed while fulfilling a terrifying and terrific feat. Take my wife for example. How many days did she spend up to her neck in blood and gore, saving lives as an ER nurse, with only her wits and her team to give her peace of mind? The calm that she has in the face of death has come from a cultivation of relaxation. She tells me that constant meditation and prayer have given her the strength to take everything in stride.

Myself, I've tended towards anger whenever I am fearful or uncertain. My knee-jerk reaction is to ball my fists. Taking a moment to re-center myself gives me the clarity to see what will be best in any situation. I know from experience that I can't always rely on my wife's calm, I can only rely on myself. It's not conceited to say this, because it is something we all have to learn. You can try it out for yourself here. The next time you are watching something that infuriates you, stop for a moment. Don't try to push away the anger. Don't try to replace it with compassion. Just stop. Look at yourself and look beyond the anger and the tornado of thought. What is at the eye of the storm? A clear view.

You can return to the clear view again and again. And remember, my goal is not to make a monk of you. My sole intention here is to ready your mind, but you cannot be ready for anything unless you are clear-minded and calm. Whenever you are faced with a serious decision, remember STOP from the First Aid chapter: sit down, think about your options, observe the pros and cons in your situation, and decide what to do. The act of lowering your blood pressure and making yourself settle is what will ultimately save your life.

Apart from fear, mental health can degrade under stress and duress. People can fall into shock even if they are not physically injured. You want to make sure you work as a unit with your family and be intimately aware of their character and any changes in mood, behavior, or temperament. Instead of thinking your teenager is just being an asshole, consider what they are going through and what they are trying to deal with. How can you alleviate the stress for them so that they can let their defenses down and relax? Furthermore, what are some of your new habits and ticks? Being aware of changes is the first step to curbing them.

Pay attention to: changes in appetite, energy levels, sensitivities and sickness, irritability or fluctuations in emotion, and unhealthy coping mechanisms like: drinking or doing drugs, smoking, or oversleeping. All of these will be indicators of degradation and you will need to take measures to build yourself or your loved ones back up. I noticed this fourth week with the Coronavirus that my wife and I started having more than a glass of wine and a beer every night. If we weren't careful, it would have been easy to make that a serious habit. We decided that we would have to drink four glasses of water a day before we could have a drink. It's a simple challenge, so it doesn't really feel like we're missing out on anything or chastising ourselves. And it makes us enjoy our alcohol more when we've "earned it". Again, the idea isn't to be self-abnegating, it's to be aware of any slips and not take them personally as you stand yourself right back up.

Here are some other tips for a stress free survival:

- **Sleep**. I asked my wife what she thinks is the leading cause of stress for the patients she's treated and she didn't hesitate to say a lack of sleep. Furthermore, a plethora of scientific evidence suggests that a lack of sleep is linked to all-cause mortality. That means you can name any leading cause of death like heart-disease, cancer or diabetes and you will find a link between sleep deprivation and symptoms. You need 6-8 hours a night, every night. I don't think I need to tell you what a good night's sleep will do for your mood, your problem-solving and your effectiveness.
- **Follow a Routine.** Do not underestimate the power of knowing what is expected of you and having meaningful work that busies your hands and calms your mind. Chores need to be done, projects need to be finished, instruments need to be practiced, games played, languages learnt. Whatever your situation, you should have a schedule for the whole household, including things you do together and apart.
- **Have family meals**. Making food together and cleaning up afterwards will bond you as a family and give you a common goal. Eating together gives you a chance to enjoy carefree

conversation. Indeed, the conversation should be light at the table. Save serious discussions for afterwards or long before. Digestion is hampered by stress, and you need to know that when you come to eat, you can just be together, it shouldn't be a strategy meeting. If you are on your own, contact whoever you can via the web, or find out more about your neighbors and offer to have potlucks at least once or twice a month. This relaxed human contact will help you to detangle from your own thoughts. It will give you a chance for a new perspective, but again, try to keep things light. You can always call people over for planning at another time.

- **Balance alone time**. Although together time is crucial, alone time is just as important if you are in a group setting. Find a safe, quiet place to read, write, practice your craft or instrument, or just be. If you are like me and your tension runs high, having eyes on you can spike your blood pressure and make you more reactive. Get your tension out with exercise or meditation, both are healthy. You do not want to trick yourself into thinking that any types of aggressive "venting" are healthy though. How many of us have put our fist through a wall because we were strung up too high and we saw no other way to get back down? Pain and suffering come from aggressive behavior. Damn, I sound like a Jedi, don't I?

- **Set purposeful and reachable goals**. If you have no hope and no end in sight, you will fall into despair. Despair is worse than fear or stress because it leaves us no option but to curl up and die. Set goals that speak to your needs, goals that you would be proud to accomplish, goals that you *can* accomplish. If you need a greenhouse built, break it down into easy steps: 1. Draw design with measurements. 2. Get materials. 3. Cut materials to size. 4. Build the frame. 5. Fill in with plastic or glass and seal. Short, simple goals are how to give yourself a fighting chance to reach your vision without slipping into that despair pit. For your family, you can discuss weekly goals, monthly goals etc. and keep yourselves culpable to those goals. Just like any gym membership, if we aren't breathing down our own neck to press on, we'll need somebody else to.
- **Exercise**. The literal connection between our mental health and our physical health cannot be overstated. You need to take time in your

day to move your body, however that is comfortable for you. Outdoor recreation will be extraordinarily valuable of course, but there is nothing wrong with walking up and down your stairs listening to an audiobook, or just doing a routine in the living room.

- **FOLLOW YOUR HEALTH PLAN**. If you or a loved one have a known condition such as schizophrenia, depression, anxiety, bipolar disorder, anti-social disorder or psychopathy, dementia, etc. Absolutely do not stray from your regimen. If you take your pills at 9 every morning, you need to know that you will have a supply to last you through the event. If you see a psychiatrist once a week, make sure you will have a means to contact them, or find a service to replace them. Do not assume you will somehow recover when disaster strikes. Assume that your condition will get worse because of the added stress and disorder. Having a condition like schizophrenia does not need to keep you from seeing what needs to be done, but as soon as you forget your prescription, or you decide you don't need it anymore, your stability and clarity will falter. It's a vicious cycle of feeling better on the medication, and then mistakenly thinking that means you're cured and then going off the meds. This depletes your brain of the chemical stabilizers and will make it harder and harder for you to ever feel stable again. I say this out of love, my own brother has been struggling with schizophrenia all his life. He was diagnosed in his twenties, along with epilepsy. He has been on a fluctuating cocktail of anti-psychotics and anti-seizure medication. Anyone who takes them knows that certain anti-psychotic medications can cause seizures, so of course my brother has had an uphill battle of leveling out his meds and every time he misses a week or he thinks he no longer needs them, he winds up in the hospital again. So please, especially in a situation where hospitals may be overworked or understaffed, keep to your regimen. If not for yourself, then for your family and all the people who truly care for you.

- **Have fun**. Never underestimate the need for free play, creativity, social interactions and down time. Fun is what gets people through hardships because it relieves the tension. Fun can be and should be incorporated into chores and projects. If you aren't enjoying what you're doing, then you'll find it becomes something dreadful and again, you literally need fun to survive. What tiger doesn't get stronger by playfighting? What squirrel doesn't get faster by chasing its siblings? Birds do usually just get dumped out of the nest, but that's not the point. We fool ourselves when we are all business. If we take everything too seriously, we're bound to become hard and unreasonable. It is easier to be calm and open because we can see clearer that way. Fun opens our eyes to novel ideas and a lightness of being that will help us survive the long-run.

I think I've said it a thousand times. You know what you need. You are only reading this book to clarify that for yourself and I hope this chapter has opened you up to possibly the most serious danger you will ever face in a survival situation. Long-term stress and duress will certainly kill you, either through a classic heart-attack, or through oversight of what is truly important. Safety comes first, of course, but that doesn't mean it isn't followed closely behind by fun, social activities, personal space, and self-care.

Chapter 8 - Recovery Work and Community Service

Let's take a moment here and reconnect to the focus of your preparations. Why are you doing all this?

_____
_____
_____
_____
_____
_____
_____
_____
_____
_____

Your answer here is sacred. It will set the stage for all of your decisions in this process. Whether you wrote: so I can stay alive and stay self-sufficient, so I can keep my family safe and fed, or so that that I can live long enough to help rebuild my community, whatever your focus is, that's what is going to guide your actions.

My purpose is to protect my loved ones and be a leader in my community during times of struggle and turmoil. I have always been a leader, but not by choice. Like many of you, I have had to lead because I have had the knowledge, the vision and the clarity to lead. It is difficult to lead because it means that we sacrifice our own wellbeing in order to make a better world for others. However, in that sacrifice is a greater sense of self, one that you can only find through service to others. You will not find yourself by hiding away in a bunker somewhere.

If I was like many of the other preppers out there, at this point I'd be telling you to fortify your land, stockpile guns, and get ready for Armageddon. But I have seen first-hand the destruction and terror that follows this kind of stupidity. I'm not telling you that there isn't a real danger from frightened people and times of scarcity and uncertainty. Of course there is. You need to use your own judgement in any situation. But this ridiculous notion that we need to arm ourselves before the other person has a chance to, and we need to strike before they do, is the kind of mentality that keeps our species in a murderous loop of fear and terror.

Arm yourself instead with a commitment to negotiate, to listen, and to cooperate. Arm yourself with the knowledge that your choice to be peaceful will encourage others to do the same. Carry a weapon if you must, but don't rush out and buy one just because some schmuck told you to. The shear amount of weaponry in my country is what has endangered us. If that sentence made you want to punch me, ask yourself this: why do you think you need a gun to protect yourself? Simple. Because the other guy is going to have one. I'm saying that as an avid hunter and owner of several guns. I'm saying that as a father of four boys, each of whom I've taught to fire pistols and rifles. When we put our faith in a weapon, we forget all the pieces that need to be in place for it to actually provide protection. Keep guns, knives, bows, bullets and whatever else you are packing, locked up. Keep it locked up and warn your children about how dangerous those things are. The most vulnerable can be put at risk when we mishandle any kind of weapon.

Okay, that's my rant. You will excuse me if I feel frustrated when I see survival experts toting weapons around like they are God's gift to America. It curdles my blood to think of what we prioritize sometimes. I want you to consider what is most important in an emergency situation: Self-isolation and self-protection? Or a collective effort to return to normality? Your decision here will not only effect yourself and your family, but also your community and the country at large.

If you chose the second option then here is what I offer: Emergency situations require heroes. Not only the uniformed kind either. We need all the strong arms to carry away the rubble. All the strong arms to carry out the dead. All the strong arms to rebuild. If you have a family or you are a caregiver of some sort, then your first job is to feed and provide for your charges and keep them safe. Your second job is to do everything in your power to help return them to a safe and stable environment.

If you are on your own, or your family is independent of you, you are exactly what the world is looking for. Setting aside your own goals to aid in the reconstruction of your community will not only make you a hero, but it will give you a sense of purpose that far outweighs any of your own pursuits.

I doubt that you wrote that your purpose for preparation is so that you can revert back to the primal stages of evolution with its focus on self-interest and survival of the fittest. We want that simplicity of life, yes, but without all the savage tendencies. Unfortunately, savage tendencies tend to rear their ugly faces when we are scared. Instead of folding in on ourselves out of fear, what can we do to feel a part of the community and a part of the regrowth?

Volunteer

The simplest thing you can do is offer your time and labour with no strings attached. Work for your friends, your neighbors, your country, and your planet. There are hundreds of movements in any given place, so a quick google search, or scan of the library bulletin boards should point you in the right direction. You can also offer yourself and your skillset to your local town and/or emergency response team and see where that gets you. I have worked in construction basically my entire life, so when it was finally time to start repairing after Katrina, I dedicated two days out of the week to recovery efforts. Of course, I still needed the high-paying jobs to keep my family afloat, but it was no trouble for my eldest son and me to drive into some of the most ravaged parts of Jefferson and help out. Even if you don't think you're strong enough to rip out walls and floors, there is always a need for coordinators, drivers, cooks, bakers, and cleaners.

Any person, regardless of their trade, can find a way to volunteer themselves to the cause. Nurses and doctors can work as medics, lawyers can help people sort through their insurance, teachers can keep children occupied and productive, grocery store clerks can help feed people, plumbers and electricians can keep relief workers from doing further damage. Whatever your strengths are, and your skillset, write them down along with a few ideas about how you can use them in an emergency situation. And remember, sometimes just being able to remain clear-headed and stable is a strength. People need someone to role model wisdom so they don't get caught up in the chaos either.

Volunteer even if it's just to care for people's animals or take livestock onto your land. Volunteer even if it's just babysitting or visiting the elderly. The rush you get from extending yourself to others is not something you can ever feel without putting yourself out there. The key is that if more people knew that they could actually contribute, then we'd have more hands on deck and the work would be far less daunting.

Join a Response Team

Communities will generally have some sort of emergency plan in place along with a team to dispatch. Find out if they are looking for volunteers (they always are). Your tasks might include neighborhood evacuations, transporting supplies and people, managing refugees, preparing businesses and homes for flooding/fire/storms, and clearing debris afterwards. I don't want to plug one task force over another, but of course, you can always join a larger organization to help with relief work around your country and in different parts of the world.

You may have some hang-ups about certain charities or organizations, so my challenge to you is to do your research and find one that you'd be proud to be a part of. And keep in mind, it's the people that make an organization beneficial. Your participation is what's going to make that association a worthy cause.

If your community doesn't have a response team, what are your options for starting one? It may be that they have lacked the leadership to create a plan and you could have an opportunity to work closely with your local council and determine a plan for evacuation, transportation, medical care, communications and management of resources and people. Remember that you shouldn't take this on alone. You should rely on expert advice and democratic solutions. However, if your area is without a plan, your effort to build one will go a long way to keeping your community safe.

Here are some tips for creating an emergency plan, and keep in mind, if you are really only trying to look out for yourself, these tips will still apply to your situation.

Step One: Risk Assessment

What sort of emergencies are likely to occur in your area, be they natural or manmade? If you live on the coast, of course you need to worry about storms, high winds, hurricanes etc., but if you are in the north, you might have flurries and blizzards, if you're on a fault line, then you might have earthquakes. People who live in tornado alley shouldn't be surprised by the cyclones outside their window. When you are looking into possible flooding, you need to assess where and when that water might come, what protections are already in place and how might they need to be revamped? In terms of fires, what protection can be added during particularly dry seasons? Risk assessment needs to be completed with all the different experts in the field: geologists and meteorologists, rangers and firefighters, doctors, scientists and the CDC. You should also scan historical papers to find out what your area has already had to contend with to get an idea of what you might face in the future.

Step Two: Establish Protective Measures

What structures are already in place to shield against a flood, fire, disease or storm? In New Orleans, the levees that were supposed to be tall and strong enough were not, so when considering your pre-existing protection, take into account that just because you have something there already, doesn't mean it will be enough. Testing is crucial to determine whether those structures will actually hold.

To bring this back to a personal level, you should have your home inspected for any old, rotting or cracked foundations. You should check your property for sinking, or flooding. Find out if your home has been rated for an earthquake if that's likely to hit. If you live by a river, find out whether you could protect your land with a dyke or with sand bags. If you live near a forest, clear a fire barrier around your house and always keep deadwood cleared away or burned. Don't store flammable materials in or near the home and mind the basic precautions about house fires: empty your lint catcher, don't overload outlets, don't use frayed wires etc.

If you are facing a pandemic like I am, protective measures include the analysis of data and the prediction of hotspots and transmission. Luckily we have a lot of data due to this world-wide phenomenon. Key points of research include: the movement of people and livestock, the incubation period of the disease and how it appears in the body, what personal protective equipment is available and who should wear it, how many beds a hospital has and what life-saving equipment they have, along with how many staff they can have on hand, and whether or not a vaccine can be made and how long that will take.

In your home, you need to consider: proper cleaning techniques, personal hygiene and distancing, mental wellbeing under stress and how you can still be effective during the outbreak without endangering yourself or others. Since this is arguably the first worldwide pandemic of our century, it has been amazing to see the sheer magnitude of cooperation between people and nations. Ordinary people have become unsung heroes because of their willingness to follow protective measures.

Protective measures can have a lot to do with regulations. What rules need to be set to keep people from making serious misjudgements? For example, during this pandemic, protective regulations like: keeping 6 feet of distance at all times, not going in public with symptoms, keeping hands and faces clean etc. all help to contain the spread of the disease. No one likes to make rules, but fair and understandable rules for your family and community will keep everyone safe. Consider what you are protecting against and make democratic guidelines that all can agree to. Also, be willing to acknowledge new procedures when new information is made available.

One issue I have found is that people have been unreasonable and unwilling to accept the new orders around COVID-19 because they were told one bit of information and they felt stuck to it, so when new information sprang up, they felt confused and incredulous. For example, there was a huge misconception about the dangers of the Coronavirus, so a lot of people did not at first pay heed to the warnings of the CDC and other organizations. Education will be key in truly understanding both the risks and the preventative measures we can take in any given disaster.

The final protective measure, which applies more to individuals and businesses than to communities is insurance. Life insurance is great for your family in the event of your death, but critical illness insurance is also an amazing investment. You can be covered for many likely diseases and injuries. This will help pay for treatment and supplement your income as well. Home owner's insurance of course has less to do with maintaining your property and more with reclaiming it. Have insurance on your home, car and business and know exactly what is covered in your plan and what you need to do to ensure you will be paid out if disaster strikes. Read through your policy with a broker or a lawyer and uncover all the fine print. You do not want to find out that flooding is considered an act of God and is not part of the agreement...

Step Three: Emergency Procedures

Each emergency is going to have its own procedure. You are not going to attempt to flee a tornado the way you would a flood. You are not going to have the notice for an earthquake that you might for a forest fire. What is most important in these procedures will be based on common sense, expert advice and circumstantial logistics, always the focus is on: keeping people alive and out of danger, ensuring all needs are met during and after the event, and then clearing and rebuilding the area.

Here are some basic procedures from my own family's plan that you can personalize and edit depending on your circumstances.

Risk Assessment: The most likely events to affect my wife and I are: Severe hurricanes and storm flooding, pandemics, house fires, and civil unrest.

Protective Measures: We have home-owner's insurance that includes repayment for damage by: storm flooding, pipe breakage, leakage, fire, lightning, smoke, explosions, and theft or vandalism. We both have life insurance policies and I have business insurance and critical illness insurance as well.

Storms: Nothing in our yard or on our home is loose or could be picked up and thrown by the wind. Equipment is kept locked in my shed. The trees in our yard are trimmed to prevent their falling on the house. The roof, windows, and doors of our home are checked every season for defects, wear and weathering and they will be replaced when there are signs of damage or weakness (my wife informs me that she has the same policy for me…).

Flooding: Our home is built about a mile from the Mississippi and a mile and a half from Pontchartrain. We have access to sandbags for added protection. We keep our home computers on the second floor and nothing important or expensive in the basement, including our food supply.

Pandemics: We keep a stockpile of food and supplies for a long-term stay in our home. My wife keeps one bag of face masks (10 masks in total) and one box (50 in total) of protective gloves in case she is asked to volunteer in an emergency (which is becoming more likely every day). We have access to antibiotics and fever-relief medication and first-aid supplies, so we do not need to go to the hospital for minor illness and injury.

Fire: Again, our yard is kept clean of flammable items, our house is far enough from the surrounding trees and neighbors' houses to prevent jumping without a strong wind. We have fire alarms and extinguishers on every level of the house.

Unrest: We live away from the city center and we can board ourselves in the home during riots. We do not make ourselves targets by flaunting wealth or advertising political or polarizing messages on our property or online. We have a network of friends and good neighbors who we can count on in times of unrest.

Emergency Procedures:

For any event, we keep connected with our emergency contact, now my eldest son, David. We also communicate with our boys and our families to ensure they know our plans and they have their own plans in place in case they are faced with anything. We stay connected with our neighbors and we make it a point to check in with them and make sure they are okay too. I communicate with my crew to ensure they have plans and they know what our options are for work and for continuity. At the moment, we are back on job sites, now that we know how to proceed with projects in a safe manner:

avoiding contact and closeness, but still being on site together to prevent injuries, not taking excessive risks around heights, machinery or electricity.

Storms/flooding: We watch the storm on meteorological websites to see its category and trajectory. We set sandbag barriers if there's a risk of the river flooding. We pay attention to the advisory warnings for evacuation. Unless the storm will be accompanied by flooding and extreme winds (>100mph), we can stay in our home. However should we be called to evacuate, we have two routes we could take to get out of the city and drive either to David's home in Mississippi or Nicole's in Texas (Amy's sister). We will take our bug-out bags and stay away from the city until the weather, the infrastructure and the social conditions make it safe to do so. We will first return to assess the damage and then decide whether or not we can stay in our home until any repairs are made.

Fire: If we have ample warning to evacuate due to uncontrolled fires, then we will take time to hose down the lawn and trees and carry away any flammable materials. We will also take our computers and some other expensive items with us when we evacuate. However, in the most likely situation the fire will be unpredictable. If it is a small one on our property, we can fight it with an extinguisher. If it spreads beyond our capabilities or if we cannot get to the extinguisher, we will leave the house immediately. We will only grab our bug-out bags if we can safely retrieve them on our way out. We will muster across the street from the home and call 911. We will not re-enter the home until firefighters tell us it is safe to do so.

Pandemic: I've discussed the procedures we've taken in great detail, so I'll explain what we would do if one of us showed symptoms of the disease, or tested positive for it. If our health was not at risk, we would BOTH remain at home in quarantine and monitor the condition for a full two weeks after symptoms dissipated. If our health was compromised in any way we would go to the hospital, warn staff of our conditions, wear protective equipment, and stay far away from other patients. We would follow the directions of staff and doctors and only exit their quarantine under their direction.

Civil Unrest: We would remain in our home, without making any unnecessary trips outdoors or into the city center. We would keep our doors and windows locked and we would not answer the door to strangers. We would stay in close contact with our neighborhood watch and utilize our home security cameras and alarms to dissuade would-be looters. If our neighborhood became unsafe, we would evacuate, taking only our bug-out bags and any small valuables that can easily be hidden. We would not want to be targeted on the road with a TV in our back seat. We would travel with Gordon out of the city and meet up at David's property. Ben and Matt would stay in Texas together.

In your own procedures, remember the priorities we discussed earlier in the chapter. First you want to keep yourselves safe and out of harm's way, then you want to focus on meeting your daily needs throughout the emergency before trying to rescue your property. Do not rush into any situation without reviewing your plan with your team and making adjustments depending on the variables like: weather conditions, road conditions and closures, access to supplies and transportation, and social disorder.

Summary and Check Lists

As you come to this final and most important chapter, I hope your eyes have been opened to the possibility that somewhere inside, you knew all of this. You may not have had the exact knowledge of how to prepare, but you were never surprised by my suggestions and nothing you read ever went over your head. Preparation is as simple as taking a stand. You say to yourself, I'm not going to live my life believing that nothing bad could ever happen. I refuse to be a victim to circumstances.

At the same time, I hope you have found that preparation is not done in fear of what might happen. It is done with a clear mind that sees all possibilities, weighs them and delivers instructions to the body to move against them determinedly. Those that can hoard years' worth of food and supplies on an acreage far out in the country are not necessarily more prepared than you, they simply had the means to make that life for themselves. Anyone living in an apartment in the middle of the city can secure their family enough food and water for a few months and lend themselves to the cause of bringing back stability to their region.

In this pandemic, I can say to you that I have seen the rainbow of humanity, some with hearts of gold, others with minds blinded in black fear and hatred of others. Our cause is to see through that all and get straight to our vision, to make ourselves available for whatever purpose that will bring order to the people. Your decision to live in wisdom instead of fear is what lead you to pick up this book in the first place and now all you have to do is one final test.

I guess by now you've noticed this isn't just a book you can read passively. It's not enough to take my word for things, you have to test them out in your experience and reference multiple sources that may be closer in relation to your own circumstance. So with that in mind, here are some questions that you can answer in order to develop your own procedures.

11. What are the possible emergencies you might face in your region?

    _____
    _____
    _____
    _____
    _____
    _____

12. Under which circumstances should you stay in your home?_____

_____

_____

_____

_____

_____

Possible answers: When it is unsafe to leave due to risk of infection, tornado or strong storms, AND evacuation has not been called. Exception: if the home is not structurally sound or protected.

13. What regulations would you and your household have in place during the emergency to stay safe?

_____

_____

_____

_____

_____

_____

_____

_____

_____

_____

_____

Possible answers: a curfew and boundary to stay within, designated muster point if they get separated, food rations, family discussions, family activities and meals, staying away from any dangerous areas: rubble, water, fire etc.

14. What supplies do you keep inside the home in case you need to hunker down there for a month or more?

___

Possible answers: include a basic list of your food and water supplies, your power sources, your medical supplies, your communication devices.

15. Who is your emergency contact, and why did you choose them?

___

16. If you were evacuated, name three places you could go.

_____
_____
_____

Possible answers: to relatives or friends out of state, to predetermined community centers or churches, or to stadiums or hotels/conference centers.

17. How will you get to your destinations?

_____
_____
_____
_____
_____
_____
_____
_____
_____
_____
_____

Possible answers: driving, hiking/walking, biking, bus/public transportation, boat etc. Include the route you would need to take for each.

18. What supplies will you and others need?

151

___

___

___

___

___

___

___

Possible answers: all of the ten essentials: food, water, shelter, first aid (remembering: medications and life-support devices), warmth, illumination, navigation, (maybe not fire or a knife), sun protection, communications, entertainment, money, a medical center, a place to sleep and to eat, protection from the storm.

19. Where do you keep your bug-out bag and what **exactly** is inside it?

___

___

___

___

___

___

___

___

___

___

___

___

_____
_____
_____
_____
_____
_____
_____
_____
_____
_____

These supplies should be checked and refreshed over time and be kept near an exit on the ground floor. For multiple family members make sure you have all ten essentials in each bag, and ensure that personal medications are included.

20. How long would you be able to stay away from home, physically, emotionally and financially speaking?

_____
_____
_____
_____
_____

21. If your family is separated where will they meet and how will they stay in touch?

22. What are your specific plans for a house fire? Include where you keep your extinguisher(s), where your alarms are located, how you would escape from any room and where you will meet.

23. How might damage be assessed and property salvaged/cleaned after the event?

_____
_____
_____
_____
_____

Possible answers: inspections will need to be completed, compromised buildings will need to be demolished or gutted, rubble can be hauled away in trucks, undamaged goods can be reused, crews can be dispatched to clear debris etc.

Author's Note:

Congratulations on completing this section of the book. It has been a joy to share my knowledge and values with you and I hope you have found this process to be rewarding as well. Return now to the pop quizzes in the introduction and determine whether or not you have secured all of those key points. Keep in mind that your preparation does not end with this book. It is crucial for you to read further into areas that I could not cover completely in this introduction. Again my suggestions are:

- Look further into growing food

- Record how long food stores actually last for you and your family and prepare accordingly
- Test out water filtration devices and water storage for yourself and if you're in an apartment, determine how you could haul water up to your floor if there was a shortage.
- Get certified in First-Aid
- Practice setting up your tent and/or building a shelter
- Practice your evacuation plan multiple times, and iron out any kinks
- Seek mental support at the first signs of stress or any changes in behavior or mood
- Find your niche in your community and become a leader in your own way

Of course, the most likely disaster we will face is one we have been slowly heading towards for as long as I can remember, that is a total global change of climate. Whether you are of the mind that this is a manmade disaster, or that it is part of a natural cycle, we can all prepare ourselves for the inevitable changes we are already seeing with the influx of large storms, extreme temperatures and wildfires. It is safe to say that we are only going to need to become more self-sufficient and collectively enlightened as we continue to navigate the weather and the social climate of our planet.

Our responsibility to look after our families is extending now to our global family. Reach out to help others and be willing to accept help too. Rely less on industry, rely less on transportation, rely less on the many things we take for granted. As many of you have lived through this pandemic along with me, I think it is fair to say that we have had an amazing opportunity to be content with less extravagance, less activity, and less entertainment.

A major point of preparation we have not spoken about is the mass migrations of people that will take place as areas become unstable due to droughts, floods, war, and corruption. What can you do to support others who had no chance to ready themselves? What is your offering to the world as we face unprecedented change? You do not have to be a martyr or a superhero, but you do have to manage your own feelings and opinions about what is to come. You do have to use your strengths and your skills to make this place just as bright as you can.

It is spring where I am and I've just planted the first seeds in my garden now. This book is my offering, perhaps the first seed that has been planted in your mind as well.

All the best to you and yours.

Printed in Great Britain
by Amazon